T5-AGB-139

RELIGION

THE DYNAMIC OF EDUCATION

RELIGION
THE DYNAMIC OF EDUCATION

A Symposium on Religious Education

Edited by

WALTER M. HOWLETT

SECRETARY OF RELIGIOUS EDUCATION
GREATER NEW YORK FEDERATION OF CHURCHES

HARPER & BROTHERS PUBLISHERS
NEW YORK AND LONDON
1929

RELIGION, THE DYNAMIC OF EDUCATION

MADE IN THE U. S. A.

A-D

*

PREFACE

THE separation of church and state is one of America's notable achievements. Education and not religion is the task of the state. This distinction has, however, made religious education a difficult undertaking. For education is a unified process, embracing the whole of life. Education in religion cannot, therefore, be complete when it is forced into a separate compartment of life and when religious training is given the child apart from the general training he receives.

As a result of this exclusive view religion has been allowed to atrophy, and to disappear to an extent from the life of growing children. And yet religion is the integrating force of life, the dynamic which gives life value. Whenever religion is allowed to drop out of education—that is, from the study of the whole of life—both the individual and the state have lost something of infinite value.

Recognizing the anomaly of this situation, some business men of New York held a meeting about two years ago to seek some solution. The leading spirit was our beloved and lamented William E. Knox. After his death, Pliny W. Williamson became the chairman of this group, known as the Committee on Weekday Religious Education of the Greater New

York Federation of Churches. Winfrey Dyer Blair is the director, and Miss Carolyn Dudley the associate.

Protestant public-school teachers, convinced of the same need several years previously, organized to meet it. They became part of the group to plan the work, electing Frank Arnold as president, and Miss Mary Newton as director.

The Brooklyn Federation of Churches, under the leadership of J. S. Carpenter, and the Hudson County Sunday School Association, under the leadership of Mrs. Mary A. Kyte, later joined in this common task. Denominational leaders, composing the Federation of Churches, also gave close study to the correlation of general education and religious education. Among these were W. P. Moody of the Presbytery of Brooklyn-Nassau, Inc.; O. V. Davis of the Presbytery of New York; Miss Louise E. Rich of the Diocese of New York; Miss Eveleen Harrison of the Diocese of Brooklyn and Long Island; and the Rev. Robert V. Russell of the Baptist Association.

Dr. Nicholas Murray Butler, president of Columbia University, was one of those pioneers who saw the serious thrust education had dealt itself in its neglect of the content and form of religion. He enthusiastically supported Professor James C. Egbert, and arranged to have the study of the problem sponsored by Columbia University Extension.

After much preliminary preparation, men and

women representing important groups in the metropolitan center of New York came together for ten Saturday mornings, to discuss this very vital problem. The papers in this volume are an attempt at least to indicate some suggested solutions.

WALTER M. HOWLETT.

CONTENTS

CONTENTS

CONTENTS

INTRODUCTION

HUGH S. MAGILL is especially qualified to speak concerning both secular and religious education. Formerly a school principal and later superintendent of schools in Springfield, Illinois, he was also for several years secretary of the National Education Association. He is now general secretary of the International Council of Religious Education and Secretary of the World's Sunday School Association. It is largely the genius of his leadership which has unified the Protestant forces in religious education and the country, city, and state Sunday School organizations into their present coöperative activity.

INTRODUCTION

By Hugh S. Magill

THE place of religion in education is a question of supreme importance. It has had the serious consideration of educators for years and is now receiving increased attention because of the emphasis that is being placed on character education in the public schools. It is recognized that religious ideals and convictions furnish the strongest sanction for sound morals; that religion is a vital element in human experience, a dynamic influence in the motivating of conduct and the determining of character, which cannot be disregarded in the processes of education.

Although the supreme importance of religion has always been recognized in America, the principle of religious liberty is held so sacred that it is quite universally conceded that religion cannot be formally taught in the public schools. Legislatures have passed laws requiring character education, and those charged with the responsibility of putting these laws into effect have stated that to make such teaching effective there must be the sanction and dynamic of religious ideals and convictions. The quality of character, which is one of the important objectives of religious education, constitutes a most valuable asset of the state. Therefore, while the state cannot furnish religious instruction, it is vitally interested in the religious training of its future citizens.

In the report of the Commission on Curriculum for Secondary Schools, published in the Sixth Yearbook of the Department of Superintendence of the National Education Association, the commission gave a very significant statement regarding the general objectives of education. To quote from the report:

> The general objectives of all education may be stated as follows:
>
> 1. To promote the development of an understanding and an adequate evaluation of the self.
> 2. To promote the development of an understanding and an appreciation of the world of nature.
> 3. To promote the development of an understanding and an appreciation of organized society.
> 4. To promote the development of an appreciation of the force of law and of love that is operating universally.
>
> The individual self, nature, society, and God—these four, and in particular the adjustments which the individual self must make—constitute the objectives of education. A full understanding of the magnitude of the task reveals the need of continuing education throughout the whole period of life. Our specific undertaking at this time is to show the part which secondary education may take in helping youth on its way from lower to higher levels of attainment.

The commission gave a detailed interpretation of the first, second, and third objectives having to do with (1) self, (2) nature, (3) society, and made the following statement regarding the fourth objective, God:

> Man craves more than a knowledge of himself, of nature, and of organized society. He hungers and he thirsts after righteousness. Knowing his own imperfections, he feels that somewhere there is perfection. The great universe calls to his spirit, and unless he ignorantly or willfully closes his ears, he hears the voice of God. No question of theology or of ecclesiastical polity is involved here. The individual soul reaches out to orient itself in the universe and to find its place of labor and of rest. No partial view suffices. Only the view of the whole, the *Weltanschauung,* will make it possible to interpret the meanings of day-by-day experience. When this orientation takes place, life assumes poise, dignity, grandeur. Otherwise its striving, its struggles, its achievements seem trivial and insignificant. No greater task rests upon the secondary school than to help its pupils to find their God. How this is to be done is the greatest of problems. Of one thing only are we sure: we cannot solve this problem by ignoring it. There is no single way to apprehend Infinity. Each in his own way may draw near.

This statement from the Commission on Curriculum, composed of many of the leading educators of the United States, is very significant. The time has come when a thorough scientific study should be made of the place of religion in education. Such a study should be undertaken by a carefully selected commission composed of leaders in general education and religious education as a contribution to the solution of this vital problem. Such a commission has been authorized by the International Council of Religious Education. The need of today is educational statesmanship of the highest order in the consideration of the relations of home, church, and state in education.

RELIGIOUS AND SECULAR EDUCATION

Luther A. Weigle, Ph.D., D.D., formerly Sterling Professor of Religious Education, now Dean of the School of Religion, Yale University, is well known among leaders in religious education. Many of his books are widely used as textbooks, including *The Pupil and the Teacher, Talks to Sunday School Teachers,* and *Training Children in the Christian Family. Training the Devotional Life* was written in collaboration with Dr. Henry H. Tweedy. Dr. Weigle takes an active interest in several religious organizations and is a member of committees connected with The International Council of Religious Education, The World's Sunday School Association, and The Federal Council of the Churches of Christ in America.

RELIGIOUS AND SECULAR EDUCATION

By Luther A. Weigle

EDUCATION and religion belong together. They have in the deepest and truest sense a common end. Education refers to the human conditions, and religion to the divine creative initiatives, which make possible the fulfillment of Jesus' purpose, when he said, "I am come that they may have life and may have it abundantly."

The full life of education and the full life of religion are bound up with one another. Education remains defective and falls short of its full end if it fails to beget the loyalty to eternal principles, the good will, the creative responsibility which enter into the making of moral character; and moral character is most surely established only when it is undergirded and sustained by a faith that the constitution of the universe itself is moral, and that moral values are therefore eternal. That faith, that conviction, is religion.

On the other hand, the full life of religion is bound up with education. A religious experience which is out of relation to one's education does not have the same promise of permanence and of fruitfulness as a religious experience which is rooted in the changing experiences and expanding powers of the passing years. A religion that attempts to do without educational methods or educational principles condemns itself to ignorance and too often to superstition.

So close is this relationship of education and religion that when for any reason they become sundered, they inevitably become rivals. Education begins to usurp the place of religion, and men in the name of religion begin to decry education. It is because of their very intimacy of relationship that this rivalry takes place, if for some reason or other they are sundered.

Education and religion are too far sundered in America today. I am thinking not simply of the fact that there are some otherwise well educated men and women who are not interested in religion, nor of the other fact that there are some who in the name of theology decry science. I am thinking of a fact that lies deeper than these—the fact that we have intrusted the education of our children almost wholly to a system of public schools, and that at the same time we have stripped these schools almost wholly of religious elements.

This system of public schools is one of the most characteristic and impressive features of American life. Over 92 per cent of the children and young people who are in the elementary and secondary schools of this country are enrolled in public rather than private or parochial schools. The amount of schooling received by the average American child has more than doubled in the last fifty years. More than that, the curriculum of public education has been greatly enriched. The public schools of today touch children's lives and influence their development at many more points than the schools of fifty years ago. The growth of knowledge and the application of science to the various fields of human industry; the development of invention, manufacturing and commerce; the social and economic changes involved in the industrial revolution and in the massing of population in cities; and the correlative changes in home life—have opened to the schools new avenues of service and thrown upon them new duties.

In the elementary and secondary public schools of the better sort today children learn not only reading, writing, and arithmetic, the languages, and the traditional subjects of literature, history, and geography, but the physical and biological sciences and their applications; cooking, sewing, and household economy; wood-working and metal-working; gardening and agriculture; stenography, typewriting, bookkeeping, and the economics of business; journalism and printing; drawing, painting, modeling and decorating; music, dancing, dramatic expression, and public speaking; physical education, personal hygiene, and the principles of public health. The fact is that under present conditions, we are relying upon these schools to afford to children much in the way of sense experience, motor training, and moral discipline which under simpler social conditions was afforded to children by the incidental contacts of everyday life in the home and the community.

Perhaps no better formula could be found to express this widening of the functions and enrichment of the curriculum of our schools than is embodied in the statement that the schools of today constitute a fairly faithful transcript or reproduction, on a small scale, of life itself. The schools are no longer mere instruments of drill in the clerical arts or transmitters of a conventional heritage of book knowledge; they constitute rather the fundamental means whereby society as a whole undertakes to reproduce itself and to shape its own progress. Education, the wisest of men have long said, is not a mere preparation for life; it is life itself. The schools of today have largely caught that vision, and are seeking to realize it in their work. The field of their activity is as broad as life. Theoretically, no human interest or occupation lies without their purview. Practically, their failure to take account of any such interest or occupation is presumptive evidence of its lack of worth or importance.

No one has done more to interpret the educational significance of the changed conditions of modern life, and to formulate ideals for the school under these changed conditions, than John Dewey. His writings on the philosophy of education have been and are of profound influence in America, and his work has more or less directly inspired the training of many of the teachers in our schools. For Dewey, education faces toward the future rather than toward the past. The end of education is not merely knowledge or power, but social efficiency, which includes, in a democratic society, the development of initiative, responsibility, and good will. Such social efficiency, Dewey maintains, can be acquired only by actual participation in the life and activities of a democratic society. It is the business of the school, therefore, to foster such a society and to induce such participation on the part of children. The school should thus be a miniature world of real experiences, real opportunities, real interests, and real social relations. It must, of course, be a world simplified and suited to the active powers of children; it must be a world, moreover, widened, balanced, purified, and rightly proportioned as compared with the particular section of the grown-up world that lies immediately without its bounds. It is a world, again, which contains a teacher who is at once leader, inspirer, interpreter, and friend. But it is a real world which reflects the fundamental, truer interests and values of the world without. Within this school world children learn by working rather than merely by listening or reading; develop originality, initiative, responsibility, and self-control by engaging in projects which call forth those qualities; and fit themselves for life by living and working together in co-operative, mutually helpful relations.

Not only has the curriculum of the public schools been greatly expanded and enriched, but our whole approach to the problems of education is being transformed. We are beginning to see the possibility of a genuinely pupil-centered organization of the life and curriculum of the schools, as opposed to the merely material-centered procedure of a generation ago. We see more clearly than teachers once did that the children with whom we deal are living a present, personal, social life, and that the measure of our success is the degree to which we fit them to stand upon their own feet with powers developed to face the problems of tomorrow.

This new emphasis upon the pupil's activity and the pupil's life, moreover, is leading to a fresh facing of the problems of character-education in the public schools. No less a term than character can be used to express the goal toward which modern educational theory is directing the efforts of the teachers of today. The term, I need hardly remind you, is not static, but dynamic. We are thinking of character not as a possession to be gained and hoarded in a napkin, but as a resource to be used. It denotes the whole body of active powers, dispositions and ideals which we seek to stimulate and develop within the growing child, who is to be the citizen of tomorrow.

Yet the strange fact is that neither the actual public schools of America, nor the ideal schools of Professor Dewey's educational theory are quite true to life. *They omit religion.* With the exception of the reading of a few verses from the Bible and the recital of the Lord's Prayer in some states and communities, the teaching of religion has disappeared from the public schools of this country; and the program and curriculum of these schools afford no conscious recognition of the part that religion has played and is playing in the life of humanity. As for Professor Dewey's theory, his book on *Democracy and Education* contains but one explicit reference to religion, and that is a reference to what the author regards as the conflict of religion with scientific interests.

This situation would seem impossible if it were not true. Yet it does not mean that the American people are indifferent or hostile to religion, or that there has been a purposed movement to take religion out of our schools. The secularization of public education has been incidental rather than purposed. It has been a by-product of the working out of the principle of public responsibility for education and the principle of religious freedom under the conditions of sectarian competition. Whenever a minority, or even an individual, has chosen to object, on what are averred to be conscientious grounds, to some religious element in the program or curriculum of the public schools, that element has forthwith been eliminated, and no other religious element has taken its place. The result of nearly one hundred and fifty years of this process has been to strip the public schools almost completely of direct religious teaching and religious worship. In some states the teachers in the public schools are afraid even to use words that have religious connotation. A year or two ago a public-school teacher was telling about the Easter season, which she described as expressive of the delights of returning spring. A child asked, "Why, Teacher, is that all that Easter means?" To which the teacher replied, "No, some people think it means more than that, but you will have to ask your father or your minister to tell you what it is." Recently in one of our great cities formal objection was made to the observance of Christmas, in any form, by the public schools; and the objection failed to be sustained only because the superintendent of schools was able to point out that the Christmas tree, the Yule log and the mistletoe have a history among the Teutonic tribes, which antedates the Christian era. The public schools of that city may still take note of Christmas because, forsooth, it is a pagan holiday! Because the religion with which certain of its symbols were once associated has been so long dead that no one can object to it.

This situation is fraught with danger. The omission of religion from the program of public education inevitably conveys to children a negative suggestion. They cannot help but notice the omission. It is bound to discredit religion in their minds. They cannot but conclude that religion is negligible, or unimportant, or irrelevant to the real business of life.

This danger is greater today than ever before just because the public schools are greater today than ever before. As the public schools enlarge their scope, the negative suggestion becomes stronger. When the public schools concerned themselves with but a fraction of life, as they did as late as a generation ago—when they did little more than drill children in the clerical arts and transmit to them a meager conventional heritage of book knowledge—when much, often the larger part, of education was gotten outside of the schools, it was of little consequence if religion was omitted from their program. But today the schools are taking on the dimensions of life itself. They provide for the education of children in practically every other sound human interest except religion. The omission, by such schools, conveys a powerful condemnatory suggestion. Today, when the work of the public schools is increasingly pupil-centered and ever more clearly directed toward the development of character, the omission of religion from their curriculum suggests irresistibly that the religious impulse should be left to atrophy, and that religion has no real bearing upon the development of character.

The principle of religious freedom which insures the separation of church and state is precious. It touches bed rock in its truth. It is a guarantee of our liberties. But the principle of the separation of church and state must not be so construed as to render the state a fosterer of non-religion or atheism. Yet that is precisely what we are in danger of doing in America today.

We must keep sectarianism out of our schools. But that does not necessitate the stripping them of religion. We must not surrender the public schools to the sectarianism of irreligion. Yet that is what in some states we are doing.

I know the customary answer. It is said that the most potent influence in the life of any school is to be found in the moral and religious character of the teacher. And we are reminded that the public schools of America are not irreligious because their teachers are almost everywhere men and women of strong moral character, and of definite religious conviction. I thank God for that. It is the one redeeming feature of the present situation. Without the definite teaching of religion, or even the mention of religious beliefs, these teachers by the character of their discipline and by the spirit which they maintain in the life of the schools, have been and are of profound influence in determining the character of American boys and girls.

But what a travesty upon the judgment and good will of the American people this situation presents. Unable to agree upon any religious principles which we are willing to make a part of the common education of our children, we shut religion out of the schools officially; then say that we will rely upon the spirit and individual initiative of the teachers.

The public schools are not to blame for the present situation. It was forced upon them. It was not infidels or atheists that stripped these schools of religion. It was folk who spoke in the name of religion. It is because adherents of all faiths in America have been more concerned to see to it that the public schools should not contain any element to which they could object, than they have been to conserve in these schools the great fundamental principles of religion and morals upon which they all agree. Protestant, Catholic, and Jew have shared in this movement. All must shoulder some of the responsibility for the situation into which we have drifted.

What, now, have we a right to expect from the public schools? Clearly we cannot expect the public schools to do the whole work or even to undertake a major share of the religious education of American children. This is for two reasons which are so obvious as to need no detailed discussion. First, because a complete religious education could not be offered by the public schools without transgressing the principle of religious freedom; second, because the growth of religion in the mind of a child depends upon a multitude of factors too intimate and too pervasive to be compressed within the limits of organized, formal schooling.

We have, however, a right to expect the public schools to do more in the way of moral and religious education than they have been doing. They can take steps to offset or wholly void the negative suggestion involved in the present situation. They can in many states continue the reading from the Bible and the recital of the Lord's Prayer—an act of corporate worship in which all religious groups might well agree to unite; and by the careful selection of materials this practice could be made to be of more religious-educational value than it now is. The public schools can and should in all of their teaching manifest due reverence for God and respect for religious beliefs. Teachers should understand that the principle of religious freedom is designed to protect rather than to destroy religious belief; and that it gives them no right either tacitly to suggest or actually to teach irreligion. The public schools can aim at the development of a citizenship which is founded upon character; and they can in their efforts to educate for character give due recognition to religious sanctions. They can teach that morality is more than custom, public opinion or legal enactment; they can point to its grounding in the structure of the universe and in the nature of God. The public schools can offset the present negative suggestion by affording to the work of the churches and synagogues for the religious education of their children some such recognition as will show to the children in unmistakable terms that their teachers realize that religion is a proper part of the community's total provision for their education, rather than a mere bit of embroidery tacked on by a few enthusiasts.

It is from this latter standpoint that the growing practice of excusing children from the public schools at their parents' request for religious instruction in church schools is, in the last analysis, to be justified. The practice is a proper recognition by the state of the fact that in education both church and state are interested, and should coöperate. It is a desirable form of recognition because it so definitely conveys to the mind of the child the suggestion that religion, instead of being the negligible thing that it now appears to be, is of important and vital interest to the school, the community, and the state, as well as to the churches.

The position which I am here taking is not popular, I am well aware, with some folk today. This opening quarter of the twentieth century has witnessed a strange recrudescence of paganism, both passive and active. In many respects the period in which we are living is remarkably like that period immediately following the Revolutionary War, during which the moral and religious life of America touched its lowest ebb. Let me take you for a moment back into that period. The Revolutionary War had fostered the growth of crime and immorality; and had plunged the country into debt and into the excesses that attend an inflation of currency. The shallow Deism of English philosophy cast ridicule upon Christianity's claim to embody a revelation of God; and the skepticism of Hume seemed to emancipate humanity from any standards other than momentary desire. "Natural right" and "state of nature," moreover, had been potent phrases in the struggle for independence. It was an easy step to exalt natural impulses and to decry the scruples of piety as unwarranted limitations upon personal liberty. Then there was France! France had been our friend and helper. France, too, was now in revolution. Jacobin clubs and societies of so-called *Illuminati* sprang up all over the country, devoted to the destruction of Christianity and the general revolutionizing of government and society. These clubs spread broadcast an edition printed in France of Tom Paine's *Age of Reason,* the foremost example of a type of popular book whose deistic affirmations were quite overshadowed by the predominant effect of the virulent, mocking negations of Christian doctrines and institutions which accompanied them.

Students caught infidelity, in those days, as they would any other fashion. The College of William and Mary, Bishop Meade wrote, was a hotbed of French politics and irreligion, and educated young men in Virginia were for the most part skeptics, if not avowed unbelievers. At Princeton, in 1782, there were but two students who professed to be Christians; at Bowdoin, in 1810, there was one. A revival at Yale had swelled the membership of the college church in 1783; but seventeen years later there were but five student members. When Lyman Beecher entered Yale as a student, he found that most of the senior class were infidels, and called one another Voltaire, Rousseau, D'Alembert, etc.

These present years are in some respects strangely like the period which I have just described. We too have been at war; and war has been followed by extravagance and by an appalling prevalence of crime and immorality. Old conventions are shattered; restraints are denounced as unwarranted repressions of individuality; liberty is confounded with lawlessness. Russia is our France; John Dewey our Hume; and Henry L. Mencken our Tom Paine. Atheism has again become blatant, and societies devoted to the propaganda of irreligion have begun to be organized. I received the literature of one such the other day, which invited me to join, not only in my own name, but in those of my children; and assured me that the children's society was being well planned, as they had secured a brilliant young girl of seventeen, living in one of the towns of Pennsylvania, to head it up and to write the lessons in atheism for the children. The desire of folk to do what they please, when they please, and where they please, finds supposedly scientific backing and sanction in the behavioristic psychology of John B. Watson, the psycho-analytic mythology of Sigmund Freud, and the free-love philosophy of Bertrand Russell. In his recent book, brazenly entitled *Education and the Good Life,* Russell frankly says, apropos of the sex education of his own children: "I shall not teach that faithfulness to our partner through life is in any way desirable, or that a permanent marriage should be regarded as excluding temporary episodes."

This, I venture to think, in spite of its present-day fashionableness among certain groups, does not represent the mind or the heart or the will of America. Underlying all our surface paganism and beneath all our differences of creed, polity, and ritual, America has, I believe, a common religious faith. Its citizens generally—Protestant, Catholic, and Jew—worship the one God, Creator of all things and Father of men. They believe that His will has been revealed in the life and literature of the Hebrew people, as this is recorded in the Bible. They acknowledge the principles of human duty set forth in the Ten Commandments, in the teachings of the Hebrew prophets, in the Golden Rule, and in the law of love to God and to fellow-man. They assent to the ideals, however poorly they may practice the precepts, of the Sermon on the Mount. They hold in high honor the character and teachings of Jesus, though only Christians call Him Lord and Saviour. They sing hymns and psalms which transcend differences of creed; and they unite in the use of the form of prayer which Jesus taught His followers.

Can we not surrender our jealousies of one another, we who profess belief in God? The need is urgent. The forces of atheism and irreligion are beginning to lay claim to the public schools as though these schools belonged to them. An at-a-distance disciple of Tom Paine has lately attempted to set himself up as a dictator, in this regard, to the public schools of the State of New York, and superparent to your children. It is one of the tragedies of our time that Protestant, Catholic, and Jew should quarrel with one another, while the real enemy of us all, the most insidious foe of American institutions, the irreligion of the day, wins its way to the minds of our children.

THE NEW EMPHASIS IN PUBLIC EDUCATION

Miss Cornelia Starrs Adair is a graduate of William and Mary College, a Doctor of Pedagogy of New York State Teachers College, and has done considerable graduate work at Teachers College, Columbia University. She has been president of the National Education Association, of the National League of Teachers Associations, and has been prominent in other educational activities. She is at present education chairman of the Richmond, Va., Branch of University Women's Clubs.

THE NEW EMPHASIS IN PUBLIC EDUCATION

By Cornelia S. Adair

A RECENT meeting of leading American educators, under the auspices of the National Education Association's Department of Superintendence, was held to consider the curriculum for the senior high schools. This conference offered a fair example of one of the most important changes which have come about in public education in the last decade. The whole trend of the discussion had nothing to do with how traditional high-school subjects should be taught. It rather centered around the question, "What are the needs of the modern American adolescent youth, and how can the public school best meet those needs?"

Modern education is going back to the example of the Master Teacher who called a little child and set him in the midst of them and said, "Whoso shall offend one of these little ones . . . it were better for him that a millstone were hanged about his neck and that he were drowned in the depth of the sea . . . for . . . it is not the will of the Father that one of these little ones should perish." The new education is child-centered. The new teacher, with greater training and inspiration, is interpreting a vital curriculum which is prepared to enable the boys and girls in our schools to achieve their highest possible development in order that they may make their maximum contribution to the communities in which they choose to spend their lives.

Back in 1918 a committee of the National Education Association, under the chairmanship of the late Clarence D. Kingsley, of Boston, issued a report on the Cardinal Objectives of Secondary Education. These seven objectives have become the new creed of the teachers of America. They are: (1) sound health; (2) worthy home membership; (3) mastery of the tools, technics and spirit of learning; (4) faithful citizenship; (5) vocational effectiveness; (6) wise use of leisure; (7) ethical character. Some of the leaders in our profession regard the seventh objective as the greatest of all. The teacher's highest goal, therefore, is to help every child achieve a well-rounded character.

You who teach in the churches also recognize the development of character as your outstanding objective. Education owes much to the church. In the Middle Ages, all schools were established by the church. Since then, civilization has followed in the footsteps of the church's missionaries, who blazed new paths and built rough houses of learning on the edges of far-off frontiers. What has been true in the development of our own country is true of other lands. Public education can never forget that the great force which you represent was the pioneer in bringing "light to them that sit in darkness."

As civilization advanced and became more complex, both church and state realized that the education of the masses must become the responsibility of the state. The reason is obvious. Equal opportunities had to be provided for all people, representing every class, creed, and nationality within our cosmopolitan American life. Our potential citizens must be brought together where they can become intimately acquainted with the various types of their fellow-men with whom they have to deal through life. Dr. Francis G. Blair has well called the public school "the American melting pot."

This change does not, however, lessen the responsibility of the church. The teaching of the public school should be supplemented by the religious teaching of the church. In order to fulfill its obligation in this respect, the forces of religious education must adopt a twofold program such as is being developed in the public schools; namely, a revision of the curriculum and the preparation of trained and inspired teachers.

In your zeal to promote week-day religious instruction, I hope you will not forget the church school, where much needs to be done. Children who study five days a week under a trained and competent public school teacher cannot be held in a church school by a teacher who is not equipped for the task. Nor will a modern school child be attracted by poorly planned lesson material.

What about the criticism public schools are "Godless institutions"? No one who really knows the situation can endorse it. As a matter of fact, the public school offers to many American children their *only* religious influence. Many parents are "so busy" that they neglect entirely the ethical and religious training of their children. You are aware that much of the material given to children in your week-day schools of religion was, in former generations, given in the home. You also know that the Bible is read daily and parts of it taught in many schools. In places where there is little or no systematic religious instruction offered by the church, the entire task rests with the public school. Dr. Edward O. Sisson, a noted professor of education, in his book on *The Essentials of Character* says, "Religion is an integral part of human life and culture, and hence of education; the great question is not education in religion, but religion in education as one of the indispensable agencies and resultants in the training of any human being."

Whenever the teaching profession speaks as a whole, it does so through its great organization, the National Education Association. Several years ago the association appointed a Committee on Character Education to set forth the work the schools are doing in that field. That committee, under the leadership of Dean Milton C. Bennion of the University of Utah, agreed that there are five outstanding objectives in character education as fostered by the public school: 1. To develop socially valuable purposes, leading in youth or early maturity to the development of life purposes. 2. To develop enthusiasm for the realization of these purposes; and coupled with this enthusiasm, intelligent use of time and energy. 3. To develop the moral judgment—the ability to know what is right in any given situation. 4. To develop the moral imagination—the ability to picture vividly the good or evil consequences to self and to others of any type of behavior. 5. To develop all socially valuable natural capacities of the individual, and to direct the resultant abilities toward successfully fulfilling all one's moral obligations.

This committee, in its final report, published in 1926, included two significant paragraphs which should be quoted here: "The school can by no means assume all the responsibility for character education. The natural responsibility of parenthood and the intimate personal relations of the home at once suggest that this institution should be the primary factor in character development. Character development is also held to be one of the chief functions of the church; but because of its present limited range of influence as compared with the schools they, the schools, may well assume responsibility next in importance to that of the home for the character training of the young. . . . Home, school, and church and all other social agencies should put forth every effort to improve the moral tone of society at large—adult society. Appeal should be made to all citizens to help this cause by their own example of good character, since this is many times more effective than precept alone." Every teacher of religion should read this report, for it bears a vital relation to the program and work of the church school as well as of the public school.

The spirit of the public school in character education was impressively set forth a few years ago by Dr. William Henry Scott, former president of Ohio State University, when he dedicated an elementary school in Columbus. He was then eighty-five years old, but the words he spoke on that occasion were full of the vigor and vision of the new day in education. He said: "Let us now, with earnest hearts and with exalted faith and hope, solemnly consecrate this building to its high and holy purpose. May the youth of this community for generations to come gather in this place to receive instruction in knowledge, and training in virtue. May they find here every condition necessary to a true and enlightened education. Especially may their teachers be examples of excellence in scholarship and character, seekers after goodness and truth, lovers of children, enthusiasts and adepts in the finest of all arts, the development and inspiration of human souls. May these rooms always be pervaded with an invigorating atmosphere of mental and moral life, and may no child pass from these schools to higher grades or to the outer world without having been made more intelligent, more thoughtful, more courageous, more virtuous, and in every way more capable of wise and just, of useful and noble, living. To this end, may the blessing of God be upon child and parent, upon pupil and teacher, upon principal and superintendent, and upon everyone whose influence will in any degree affect the work of education as it shall be conducted within these walls."

What is the school doing in the field of character education? Let me give a few specific examples. Some eighteen or nineteen years ago a boy was born in a Western city. While still a baby he contracted infantile paralysis, which left one limb badly crippled. A little later he lost both father and mother and was placed in a home for orphans, where he learned to hobble about on his crutches. One day there came to the orphanage a workingman and his wife who wanted to adopt a child. They told the superintendent they wanted a little boy who was bright, strong, and healthy. The superintendent took them to see the children, but when the wife saw the lame boy she suddenly changed her plans. The boy went to his new home and later to the public schools. He passed on, finally, to the high school, where he was discovered one day by the superintendent, who was attracted by the boy's unusual face. The superintendent persuaded local business men to finance an operation, and the lad soon became able to walk without crutch or cane. But he was a dreamer. He had strange and beautiful thoughts. The superintendent urged the teachers to encourage those thoughts, and he began to write them down. They were brought to the attention of the other pupils, and the boy who had been a cripple and a dreamer became a class favorite.

The high school had always been interested in athletics and the president of the senior class was usually an athlete. But in the senior year of the boy of whom I speak, the star athlete of the school rose in the senior class meeting and said: "We have an unusual opportunity this year. We have learned in this high school that character and scholarship count in life. There is a boy in this class who has led in both, and I move that we elect Jimmie Williams as president of the class." The lame boy, who was a dreamer, became president of the class. When the class yearbook was being prepared, the editor asked their president to write a foreword, and his message took the form of this prayer:

"Great Father, others have been strong and confident,
  They, too, have had their wispy, star-dust dreams.

To them, the world has seemed a flowering continent
  That bloomed in life's invigorating beams.
And we who are as they were, look for them today.
  Oh, Father, with their sterling visions, where are they?

Blind giants swing their axes, chopping grass
  Within a wood of oaks. Swift ships from storm-raked
    seas
Have lost their figureheads and, drifting, pass.
  A racer prays for speed, but stays upon his knees.

Yet, if this is the end of those who dream and hope,
  We still shall smile and challenge all the world.
For man is always puny in his visions' scope,
  And dreams are marching-banners, never furled.
Our own horizons are a never-ending call.
  Oh, Father, may we answer well before we fall."

At a meeting of the National Society for the Study of Education recently held at Dallas, Texas, Professor Harold Rugg, of Teachers College, Columbia University, thrilled an audience with his account of the character-education experiments he has conducted in the Lincoln School in New York. He gave a new realization of the need for developing self-expression in the children by means of what he calls "freedom with control and disciplined initiative." Mr. Rugg then read these lines, written by a pupil in the junior high school:

"I went to church one day,
  And God sat by my side,
  And we laughed at the people

With their prayer-books,
Saying prayers to a God so far away.
'Heaven is pearl-paved,' said the preacher,
'And gold, and the angels sing
His praises on their harps.
It is there that you and I
Will some day go.'
And God laughed and said to me,
'Heaven is a broad field
And a brook.
And the lean, scarred, beaten horse
And the houseless cur
And the hunted deer
Will go there with me.' "

Public schools which give their pupils guidance and encouragement and freedom for self-expression such as these two cases are surely not "Godless." Professor A. C. Purdy, of Hartford Theological Seminary, speaking before the National Education Association's Department of Deans of Women in 1925, said the greatest desire of modern youth is self-expression. There is no institution in the world to-day which is meeting that need more adequately than the public school. Without the guiding influence of mature minds, such as that provided by teachers, young people would express themselves in channels harmful to themselves and others.

This self-expression of the public-school pupil is, however, not confined merely to the writing of poetry. Two years ago, the schools of Birmingham, Alabama, adopted as their year's slogan, "The Development of

Character Through Work." The previous year, the slogan had been "True Sportmanship." The school recognizes that the urge for physical conquest, so strong in adolescent youth, must be satisfied. It also realizes that in the expression of that instinct lies a character-building opportunity. After the Birmingham schools had devoted a year to encouraging true sportsmanship, they stressed the nobility of honest work. An industrial leader, speaking to the teachers of that great Southern city, said, "What concerns industry most regarding the schools is the attitude of their product toward work. Technical information, although of great value, is much less important than a wholesome attitude toward work and social obligations."

A few years ago, educators argued about the method of teaching morals, or ethical character. Some said it could not be taught at all. At the other extreme were those who thought the schools should introduce regular courses in morals. Now we find that the lessons of character are effective only as they are taught in relation to all the activities of life. Thus character is being taught through the media of the regular school courses—mathematics, literature, science, history, physical education, and the others.

We, therefore, affirm that the great American public-school system is making a decided contribution to the advancement of our civilization through the teaching of ethical character. The teachers of the American public schools wish religious educators Godspeed in their task of definite training in religious living. We are coworkers. Our task is illustrated by an incident which occurred a few years ago in the city of Washington. On the highest point of the District of Columbia is being erected a great cathedral of the Protestant Episcopal Church. One day a stone-mason, at work on the cathedral, entered the office of one of the canons to tell of the death of his wife and to ask that she be buried in the cathedral. His request was denied because the cathedral vaults are set apart for only the bodies of *distinguished* Americans. A few days later the stone-mason returned and said: "I have buried my wife in the cathedral. I had the body cremated, and this morning I carried the ashes up here to Mount St. Albans and sprinkled them in the mortar that we place between the stones. She is buried in the cathedral!" In generations to come, pilgrims to Mount St. Albans will see the completed cathedral, but few will know that helping to support its stately walls are the earthly remains of an unknown woman whose husband put into his work that which he loved above all else.

You and I are building a new America with the youth of today. Let us together put into our structure the finest material we have. The spirit in which this is to be done was well expressed by a schoolteacher, Miss Caroline Woodruff, of Vermont, in a poem entitled, "My Trust":

"I am a teacher—
And trusting, childish eyes
Look unto me confidingly,
Their little hands in mine,
To follow me to anywhere.
Be my way on high or low or middle ground,
They follow.
Oh, let me feel
What mighty trust is mine!

I am a teacher—
And ardent, restless, longing youth
Look unto me expectantly,
Fulfillment of their dreams to aid,
As I lead they follow.
Oh, let me take the upper road
Leading to the heights,
And they must follow.
A mighty trust is mine!

One there was
Known throughout the ages,
And over all the world—
The Great Teacher,
Who leads forever to the Light.
His name I bear.
Oh, wondrous thought
That challenges my highest, best.
I am a teacher."

RELIGION ESSENTIAL TO GOOD CITIZENSHIP

JOHN J. TIGERT, M.A., Ed.D., LL.D., is the author of such books as *The Philosophy of the World War, The Child—His Nature and His Needs,* and *The Book of Rural Life* and of many articles in leading periodicals. His experience has been varied. He was professor of philosophy in Central College, Missouri, and in the University of Kentucky; president of Kentucky Wesleyan College. Since 1921 he has been United States Commissioner of Education.

RELIGION ESSENTIAL TO GOOD CITIZENSHIP

By John J. Tigert

PROFESSOR W. R. WEBB, familiarly known as "Old Sawney," founder and principal of the famous Webb School of Bellbuckle, Tenn., who recently passed on after a half century of influence upon education in the South unsurpassed by any of his contemporaries, used to say frequently, "A boy is a bundle of possibilities." This favorite phrase of "Old Sawney" might well serve as a fairly literal, though homely, translation of the etymology of the word "education," being, as it is, an abstract term derived from the Latin *e,* "out," and *duco,* "to lead." Education, in the proper sense of the term, must include the highest possible realization, the most complete, harmonious, and symmetrical perfection of all the potential powers inherent and innate in man's nature. Education is the process of cultivating to the fullest flower all the seeds that lie implanted in this wondrous composite of mind, soul, and body.

The tendency has been strong among professional educators to emphasize the development of mental powers as the proper function of the educative process, frequently to the exclusion of other capacities of the soul and body. It must be granted that the emancipation of the mind should be the chief function of the institution of learning, that the growth of spiritual power should be the major concern of the church; but likewise it must be agreed that the making of strong bodies is at least a secondary function of the school in view of the oft-quoted dictum of Juvenal, *Mens sana in corpore sano.* But while the realization of mental possibilities is the prime objective of the school, it is unfortunate that certain prejudices have tended to exclude proper regard for the attention to the soul and body. Perhaps the neglect of the former has not been due so much to prejudice as to a feeling that this is a function of the church and the desire to render to God the things that are God's, retaining for Cæsar only the things that are Cæsar's.

This is certainly true, I think, in the case of the public schools and all those institutions supported by public taxation, because it is evidently the fear of many that the effort to teach religion in publicly supported schools and colleges may lead to an indirect violation of the cherished American doctrines of religious liberty and separation of church and state. Be that as it may, it is probable that we can agree upon a distinction of function in the church and state and admit the wisdom of the founders of the Republic in recognizing this distinction; in fact, this is one of the most salient contributions that American statesmen have been able to make to political progress in the world. The late Bishop E. E. Hoss set out the difference in the function of church and state in these words: "Secularity is the badge of the state. The sphere in which it moves and acts is the sphere of visible and tangible things. It has no eye for the eternal realities. Its symbol is the sword, for it may use force. The church, on the other hand, is the vehicle of religious truth. She has a message to deliver that the state has no voice to convey. Her symbol is the shepherd's crook, and she dares use no instrumentality except persuasion."

Though there may be some justification for the neglect of the soul in public institutions of learning, yet no adequate excuse can be assigned for a certain prejudice that has existed with reference to physical education. Fortunately, this prejudice seems to be disappearing. Much improvement has come in our schools in health and physical education during the past few years, due largely to the revelation that approximately one-third of American young men proved under examination to be physically unfit to bear arms in defense of their country. It is strange that we should have so long neglected the proper concern for the care of the body upon which the welfare of the mind is organically conditioned and with which the culture of the soul is intimately connected, if we accept the oft-quoted and much-approved doctrine of John Wesley, "Cleanliness is next to godliness."

Aside from the question of the peculiar functions of the school, the church, and the state, these organizations are all joint agencies in the promotion of the greatest possibilities in our youth for individual and social welfare. In its widest connotation, education is the result of all the forces which affect the life of man. Taken in this sense, religion is the most universal element in education as well as a very powerful stimulus to human action.

We hold, first, that the religious element is universal. By religion we mean the consciousness of some kind of communion between man and a supernatural Being, a Deity, or God. We have had many arguments set up to establish the existence of such a Being: ontological and anthropological arguments, arguments for a first cause, for design, and others. Whether any or all of these arguments which have been advanced in proof of the existence of a supernatural Being could convey to those altogether destitute of the idea of the Deity, first the notion of God as a person self-existent, eternal, immutable, of infinite power, wisdom, and goodness, the creator and upholder of all things, and, secondly, satisfactory proofs of his existence, is a question which it is impossible to settle and which we would not find profitable to discuss here. We shall not raise the question of the possibility of philosophical or logical demonstration of the existence of God. We shall assume for our purposes the famous dictum of Professor Calderwood of Edinburgh, "The reality of the Divine existence is a truth so plain that it needs no proofs, as it is a truth so high that it admits of none." It is worthy of note, however, and sufficient importance has been attached to the fact, that the conception of a supernatural Being has apparently always existed in the mind of man, wherever and whenever we have had knowledge of him. This is evidenced not only by the ancient writings of the Jews, but by the earliest historical remains and the extant beliefs and customs of all peoples, Asiatic, African, American, European, and Polynesian. We cannot show that the ideal of God has always existed in the mind of man from man's inception, but we can show that all men known to history have possessed the idea of God. Once projected within the sphere of human knowledge, from whatever source and in whatever manner, this notion of God, however abused, has never been permitted to perish. This does not, of course, necessarily mean God with all the personal attributes ascribed to him by Christians; but it does mean the belief in supernatural power of some kind, whether in the fetishism of the savages of all parts of the world which attributes extraordinary powers to sticks, stones, herbs, images, the sun, the moon, and other inanimate objects; in the polytheism of the Greeks, Romans, and others, who personified and endowed with magic qualities the forces of nature; or in those, like the Chinese, who have worshiped the spirits of departed ancestors.

It is not only true that the notion of God exists and has existed in all species of mankind known to us, but it is likewise true that the notion has everywhere been a powerful force, if not actually the most powerful force, operating in the lives of men. In every form of communion with the supernatural, the notion of the Deity has been sufficiently powerful in its influence upon man to move him to make the supreme sacrifice of his own life or the lives of those dearest to him. We witness this in the most primitive form of religion, in fetishism, where parents appeased the spirit of Moloch with the burning of their own offspring, or where the Indian mother adores the alligator by throwing her babe into the sacred waters of the Ganges. We witness it in the polytheism of the Hellenic peoples, as in the cult of Artemis. Iphigenia is sacrificed by her father, Agamemnon, to appease the goddess, so his fleet may sail for Troy. We witness it in monotheism, in the blood of the countless Christian martyrs, and in the sacrificial death of Jesus Christ upon the Cross for the conciliation of God and the redemption of mankind. There certainly has been no more impelling motive in the life of man than his belief in the Deity.

Again, we think that sufficient significance has

not been attached to the fact that among the great thinkers who have interpreted reality and who have explained the origin and the meaning of the cosmos, almost without exception these philosophers have required the notion of the Deity to make the universe possible, intelligible, or thinkable. Those few who have not required the Deity for an explanation of the universe do not loom up among the great figures in the history of philosophy. Among the Greek philosophers we have atheists such as Democritus and Leucippus, but they sink into insignificance as compared with such theists as Pythagoras, Socrates, Plato, Aristotle, and others. We do not recall an outstanding atheist to match against the cloud of theologians and schoolmen of the Middle Ages. Among the moderns, Diderot and the so-called French encyclopædists, a few Germans, including Haeckel, a small number of Englishmen, and others who compose the atheistic schools of thought are hardly recognized within the pale of philosophy in a large sense. As over against these stand Descartes, Leibnitz, Spinoza, Locke, Berkeley, Kant, Fichte, Hegel, Lotze; in America, James, Bowne, Ladd, and a whole host of others who include within their number the great names of modern philosophy, who have grappled seriously with the explanation of this world and who have traveled many paths, but have all reached the same destination—God.

If education consist in the evolution of the man's

inherent capacities or untying "the bundle of possibilities," to return to Mr. Webb's figure; if religion be a universal phenomenon among men; and if great thinkers find God indispensable to the explanation of reality—then education which lacks the religious element is certainly seriously defective.

The great world catastrophe through which we have passed has started many anxious inquiries and has awakened deep misgivings on the part of some. Speculation is openly engaged in as to whether civilization can be salvaged, whether war will destroy civilization or civilization will destroy war. There is much pessimism abroad in the world, and we are passing through critical times. Crime of all kinds, divorce, and immorality have greatly increased among us. There has been a disregard of the rights of others, a social discontent, an industrial unrest, a menace of radicalism, an unbridling of vice, and a growing disrespect for the law that has never before characterized our country to the present degree and which arouses the concern of every true American. If these observations be correct (and I think that few will demur), which way shall we move to correction? Where shall we find the remedy for these conditions and how shall we proceed to apply it?

Enlightenment and better understanding will undoubtedly help the situation, but these cannot save us. If the war teaches us any one lesson more clearly than another, it is the insufficiency of culture, knowledge, and science *per ipsos* to promote the welfare of mankind. Germany claimed a *Kultur* superior to any that the world had known at the outbreak of the war. She was not excelled by any other people in the great fields of science, philosophy, music, and commerce. A degree from a German university was highly coveted above a degree from one of our own institutions. Illiteracy was at an irreducible minimum among the German people. They enjoyed a high degree of general enlightenment and a fairly homogeneous population. But what was the result of it all? Germany's strength in philosophy, in science, in industry, and in other respects contributed to the ruin of a great people and involved the world in the most titanic tragedy of the ages. A weaker nation would hardly have risked the wrath of the world, even though it had been moved to fly at its throat. But Germany's consciousness of great power gave her the confidence to attempt the impossible.

German political philosophy convinced her that democracy was the symbol of weakness, chaos, and incompetency in government; that the German people were chosen by God to exterminate weaker peoples so that a race of supermen might be evolved. German science, applied to the arts of war, convinced her that she could defy the world; applied to undersea craft, she could sink unsinkable ships like the *Lusitania;* applied to aircraft, she could terrorize London and Paris and spread disease and destruction among her enemies; applied to nocuous gases, she could blind and wipe out armies in the twinkling of an eye; applied to cannon, she could crush the impregnable forts of Liége like eggshells and hurl projectiles a distance of seventy-five miles into Paris. German commerce and industry convinced her that she must expand through middle Europe into Asia and Africa and dominate the world. German music convinced her that hymns of hate were of more force than hymns of love. Germany's faith in her "divine mission" and the consciousness of the necessity of fulfilling it convinced her that treaties were "mere scraps of paper to conceal political purposes." Harnack, whose theology and views with reference to the Bible probably carried more weight in America before the war than any other scholar's, became one of nearly a hundred leading savants of Germany who convinced themselves that the violation of Belgium was just and good. It is hardly necessary to recite further the history of Germany's folly, but the world has never before had such an exhibition of the inadequacy of mere philosophy, science, industry, and things secular. Plainly, these things can be both evil and good, hurtful and helpful, undesirable and desirable, the hope and the menace of civilization.

The value of man's progress in knowledge turns upon the will or judgment of those who may possess it. In the hands of the physician, even poison has its benefit; in the hands of the pioneer, knives, axes, and guns are of immeasurable value; but who would claim that these articles were good for babes or thieves? Education which devoted itself entirely to the discovery of knowledge, without regard for the will or intention of man, is likely to prove the undoing of society. Certainly it is not worthy to be called education. Surely, after the demonstration of the ruin that lurks in the wake of mere emancipation of the mind, we must see that there is a great truth in the words of Bourdillon:

> "The night has a thousand eyes,
>   And the day but one;
> Yet the light of the bright world dies
>   With the dying sun.
> The mind has a thousand eyes,
>   And the heart but one;
> Yet the light of a whole life dies
>   When love is done."

How shall we direct the will and train the heart as we enlighten the intellect? Naught but religious feeling, the inspiration of the soul, and faith in God can accomplish this. Even ethical teaching and morality, though helpful, will not suffice. Moral philosophy may be similar to other knowledge, the product of man's mind, but not a force which controls his acts. There are abundant examples of the failure of ethical teaching to affect life. France has given non-religious moral training a more thorough trial, perhaps, than any other nation. And yet, says an eminent authority, "In fifty years criminality has increased threefold, though there was scarcely any increase in population." This statement was made before the war and does not comprehend the violent increase of crime since the war. One French professor complained, "My prize pupil in morals is the biggest knave of the lot."

Let no one suppose that I am opposed to the teaching of morals in the schools. On the other hand, I strongly advocate it. Recently I emphasized the need of instilling virtue, honesty, and integrity through our schools. I believe in beginning early the relation of stories of moral import, the recounting of golden deeds of kindness, and the teaching of virtue in every possible way to our children.

But this moral instruction requires the reënforcement of religious teaching and feeling. The church becomes the supplement of the school for this purpose. In private, parochial, and church schools, religious instruction can be given with secular teaching, but cannot be given in publicly supported institutions. The public schools at Gary, Indiana, Toledo, Ohio, and a few other cities are working out a system in which the schools become a community center surrounded by churches of all denominations, to which the children go regularly from the public school for religious instruction. Some state universities are working out a system which is similar in principle. We have numberless instances of the powerlessness of knowledge to make men good. The age of the Italian Renaissance, a new revival of learning, was likewise an era of immorality and loose living. Pope described Bacon as at once "the wisest, brightest, meanest of mankind." Solomon, the wisest of all the kings, was by no means the most virtuous. Rousseau, a great name in the history of education and philosophy, gives us his ideal training for Émile and dwells especially upon the value of his moral code, meantime neglecting shamefully the rearing of his own child and engaging in dissolute living. His confessions are amazingly frank, but even they do not uncover the vileness of his life. Morality is indeed the worthy helpmate of religion, but history and experience reveal over and over again that it cannot be substituted for it. Ethical societies have failed to supplant the church.

I am well aware that the position I take is not popular today among certain people, and that some will say that it is a poor philosopher who cannot discover salvation by logic and reasoning. My reply is that of the "Fable of the Chicks," if I may be pardoned for recalling a parable told by my departed father. He related the experiences of two chicks that happened to be companions in the same setting. The hen had been sitting for nearly three weeks on the eggs and the time for them to hatch was almost at hand. One chick was stirred by instincts of a world of greater freedom beyond the white walls that inclosed him. He soliloquized, "I feel that outside there is another world in which I shall find air, sunshine, and food. I feel that these wings and legs will come into play and I shall be happier there. And yet I do not know that this is true. Further, I cannot act upon any assumption that cannot be known and logically demonstrable. I shall not be swayed by foolish sentiment. I shall not break this shell." Just beside the egg that contained this agnostic chick, another chick was soliloquizing, "I, too, feel that outside is a world of greater freedom, where I can run and fly and where I shall enjoy the air, the sun, food, and water. I do not know that such a world exists, but I have faith that there is and I cannot resist the feeling that impels me to pip this shell. I shall pip my shell today." A few days later, the busy housewife discovered the hen with the brood of chicks, but in the nest lay one egg. It was cold. She broke it with her thimble. There was a cold and lifeless form. It was our agnostic philosopher who could not act upon faith, but acted upon the dictates of his reason.

THE CHURCH'S RESPONSIBILITY IN EDUCATION

The Reverend J. V. Moldenhauer, D.D., is collegiate pastor of the First Presbyterian Church in New York City. He came to this church from the Westminster Presbyterian Church of Albany, New York, where he was pastor for several years. He delivers many lectures on church history and biblical literature.

THE CHURCH'S RESPONSIBILITY IN EDUCATION

By J. Valdemar Moldenhauer

MAY I suggest, in a very informal way, a contrast between the past and the present, in order to make amends for some of the things that have been said and assumed by the present with respect to the past. I hope that you are all as fond of Mark Twain as I am. You recall the time when, for the only occasion in his hectic and many colored career, Tom Sawyer posed as a model church school scholar. In the simple community in which he lived boys and girls in the church school were rewarded for proficiency in their lessons by receiving little tickets of various colors, and these tickets were saved and exchanged for those of higher denomination and different hue as progress was made. A great occasion was approaching at which the church school was to be tested by a superior person who was to find out who were the brightest scholars and what they had done. Tom was very short of tickets, but very long on resourcefulness. He conceived the idea of buying up tickets, and so he bargained for them, exchanged the impedimenta in his pockets for tickets, and soon possessed an unbelievably large assortment. On the great day he presented himself, and since, to use the political phrase, there was no going behind the returns, he had to be accepted on the face of the very fine showing he made. He was called to the front of the church schoolroom and there he was questioned by an urbane, self-conscious, and dignified person who was present to show off the school. Tom was urged to give a sample of his wares. He was urged to show how much he knew about the Scriptures. But Tom proved hesitant, and only when the urging had become so sharp that he was unable to resist was he persuaded to answer a question. The great man asked him who were the first two disciples. Tom replied, "David and Goliath." Mark Twain very properly draws a veil of charity over the rest of the scene.

I suppose that many of us have almost made up our minds that the old church school process in its whole history was quite as inefficient, if not as delightfully humorous, as is suggested by this episode. In fact, there are many persons who, in talking about the church school work of the past, would have us believe that it was by something more than the miraculous grace of God that any of us escaped the corruption of a complete and abysmal ignorance.

The past certainly had its troubles and inefficiencies, its days and sometimes years of getting along with imperfectly trained teachers and certainly very badly adapted surroundings; but we who live in what we assume to be a much better day ought never to fail to appreciate that which was perennially good and lovely in that older time. We shall prepare ourselves very poorly for the work which we have to do unless we have in our minds a humble thankfulness for the good as well as a reasonable criticism for the imperfect. We should have the deepest gratitude for the devoted hearts that in conditions extremely difficult and in circumstances unsuited to adequate training made so great and so devoted a contribution to the task of teaching the children of the Christian church the religion of their Lord and Master.

Yet recent years have brought a tremendous development. That past has gone and we are aware of problems and phases of work unknown to those early days. We are now self-consciously undertaking the task to which we no longer assign the simplicity which we once supposed it to have. That much has been learned about the action of the human mind is a fact which should be recognized even by those who are most cautious in their acceptance of all that is said in the name of psychology. In fact, our increased understanding of the difficulties involved in teaching the child counsel us to approach the whole problem of religious education in our church in a way that is fairly new.

Some principles are now accepted as imperative. First, every church that has given any serious thought to the question of religious education insists that the church is responsible for the expense incurred in carrying on this work among the children and young people. It is hardly necessary to argue that the church should properly maintain its institutions of religious education, rather than have it supported by the old simple system of making the children themselves bring their pennies and nickels and pay for their own religious education. We have put the support of the church school in the church budget. Some churches say that their expenses are such that it is out of the question to adopt such a plan, but they admit that it is the proper way.

Another principle is that there ought to be an adequate physical equipment for the work of the church school, the maintenance of which is just as much a responsibility of the church as that of the proper beauty and fitness of the place of public worship. In the old days it was supposed to be altogether right to let the church school get along as best it could. I well remember being told, when I came to my former parish, about its wonderful primary department. It met in a large hall and was taught by a very capable woman who for many years kept the department together. I do not deny that she probably did a very fine work, but it was done in the teeth of physical difficulties which no self-respecting church has a right to force upon the experience of persons who are devoted and intelligent enough to teach in the church school.

One other principle is that our teachers should be well trained. We are increasingly hesitant about accepting for the work of our church school a teacher, no matter how well intentioned, who is not willing to undertake a certain amount of study, either private or in training classes, so as to become equipped for the task with a better understanding of children and of what is taught them.

A final principle which many as yet are slow to accept is that the training of our children should be directed by persons who are specially trained. This at once suggests the idea of expert leadership in religious education. In this connection two or three things should be stressed.

In the work of expert leadership we need to maintain a decent sense of the comparative value and size of things. This is sometimes referred to as a sense of humor, which often helps in situations where nothing else can do as much. I regard humor of this sort as a real gift of God, and I have often wondered just how some of these difficult and new tasks can be carried on by persons who are lacking in it. I have a friend, a physician who has a sardonic wit, who made a remark at the time of our entrance into the World War, when the newly recruited soldiers were being fitted with all kinds of misfit clothing: "I don't know what they are all quarreling about. Those shoes and those suits are all right. The only trouble is that those boys are all the wrong shape and the wrong size." The person who is beginning a new order of things has often to remember that the Procrustean method is not the most effective.

The other side of the matter has to do with the church, its members, officers, and pastor, and their attitude toward persons who undertake expert work. They sometimes behave as a shy child in the presence of a stranger. A skeptical or suspicious state of mind on the part of a church group toward the director of religious education may cause serious difficulty. The members of a church where such new work is inaugurated should exercise two qualities. First, they must show respect to the expert. Of course, though there are two popular definitions of an expert, the one "an ordinary man away from home," the other, "one who knows more and more about less and less," capability is really altogether admirable. And secondly, the divine gift of patience ought to be exercised. We are not to expect miracles in an age when miracles, according to good Protestant teaching, have not been happening for some time.

Passing from these preliminary considerations to what I conceive to be the main purpose of Christian religious education and of church schools, I suggest the following: It is essential that the church should know what it is doing in the sense of knowing what it is aiming at, namely, the training of the child in the personal and social experience of true religion. We are training the child to know the sense of the presence of God in his own life. We are teaching him to realize his necessary attachment to those who in association with him have a common experience of God. And we are instilling in him the eagerness, by himself and with his brothers, to make the sense of the presence of God the real motive in the life of men everywhere.

This is indeed the old and simple threefold division of the Christian gospel, personal religion, the love of the church in the sense of attachment to the community, and the interest in applied Christianity generally. I hold that we should instruct our children during church school periods in all these phases of the Christian life so that when they grow up they will not regard any of them as unusual or unreasonable. One of the unfortunate features of the life of our church today is that many who have been brought up in the Christian church have developed a kind of religion that takes a few things for granted, but leaves them unprepared to see anything beyond. For example, there are many who regard it as religious to say the Lord's Prayer, sing hymns, go to church, and conform to customary moral standards, but who feel a strange and inexplicable unwillingness to accept the truth that Christianity must be brought into a hitherto untouched situation. They think that religion is being departed from if anyone suggests that belief in Christ means to apply what we believe about Christ to what is present in a contemporary world situation. There are those who hold themselves to be good Christians who are annoyed and sometimes angry if the minister devotes a sermon to prove that one's Christianity must be manifested in such a project as doing away with war. They have never had it ingrained into their consciousness that the Christian religion signifies that everything that Christ meant should be made a part of the life of the whole world.

It is also essential that the church should know where, for the purpose of training its young, is the main source of its knowledge and inspiration. We hold that this source is the Bible. That does not mean that we should neglect or despise any chapter of the life of mankind's religious experience. It does mean that standing where we do in this age of the life of Christendom, we are perfectly well assured that the main stream in which this inspiration of mankind has flowed is the Bible. It matters not at all that outsiders keep asking with evident irritation why we should care so much about what has happened to the Hebrews. Would one race be picked out, one little insignificant nation, to convey a universal revelation? Is there anyone who thinks you have scorned the rest of the history of mankind because you state the obvious fact that the greatest flowering of the genius of man in the appreciation of beauty and the power of creating beauty was in ancient Greece between the years 550 and 300 B.C.? If you ask why this happened in Greece alone, I say I don't know how it happened, I simply know that it did. So when one asks how it can be possible that God should have given his supreme revelation to just one people, I answer, I do not know, but he did.

This is the Bible with which we have to deal, and it is a pitiful thing that there should be a tendency to show disrespect for the great source of our teaching concerning the meaning of life in Jesus Christ. Do not let it be understood that I am forsaking my long-held position with regard to perfect freedom in the study and exposition of Scripture. I am not going back on my convictions about the critical study of both the Old Testament and the New. The critical process in the interpretation of Scripture has on the whole yielded good results. We have learned that the Bible can be taken on the basis of the most complete restudy, and all the more be found to offer us that light of life which we need and which we wish all men to have.

Now if the Bible is to be the source of religious education there are one or two assumptions that have to be made. We shall have to assume a degree of interest in the work itself, in the children, and in the Bible on the part of two sets of people. First, the people in the homes from which these children come. I would like to have every parent made uneasy about that. It is depressing to realize that often a child goes home from a class where the teacher has been interesting and instructive to meet an atmosphere which is completely dull and uninterested with respect to the whole question—an attitude of such total indifference that if he were to see his father or his mother reading a Bible, the poor child would not know what to make of it. Certainly our best work cannot be done so long as there is lacking that interest in the home.

But inside the church itself we have the same necessity for a continued interest not only in the work, but in the Bible itself. I think that ministers have too often been to blame. Why should a pastor assume that there will always be an intelligent interest in the Bible on the part of church-school teachers and pupils when he himself has never taught them anything about the Bible? It is no less gratuitous to assume that the interest in the work of the church school will continue where the leading members of the church do not take an interest in it. Those of us who have been so circumstanced that we could always be intimately associated with the work of the school, have found that one of the most painful things church-school workers have to fight against is the indifferent attitude of nine-tenths of the church members toward their work. How can we expect that the real meaning of the Bible and of the Christian life can be instilled into the children where this attitude exists? There are people in the church who never see the church school except on those Sundays when the church school comes to church to present a pageant or engage in some other public "exercises."

The responsibility of the church in religious education is such that it cannot be evaded without dishonor and increasing helplessness. A church that refuses to assume its responsibility will have no right to complain if it discovers growing up about it a generation ignorant of its gospel and indifferent to its claim. But a church that accepts the burden imposed, with a cheerfulness undiscouraged by the threat of inevitable difficulties, will make the happiest of all discoveries, and that is that the old gospel is really new with a perennial freshness that expresses itself naturally and easily in new methods and new words.

THE BIBLE IN EDUCATION

WILBERT W. WHITE, PH.D., D.D., is president of The Biblical Seminary in New York City. With the exception of two years in the pastorate, Dr. White has devoted his life to the work of teaching the Bible. He was professor of Hebrew and Old Testament literature in Xenia Theological Seminary, and of Biblical Literature in the Moody Bible Institute, Chicago. He is also the author of several volumes of Bible exposition.

THE BIBLE IN EDUCATION

By Wilbert W. White

WE CAN put the Bible into education, once we really believe it to be worth while to do so. To the worth-whileness I address myself.

The Bible is the product of the highest type of education. An amazing amount of the finest physical, mental, social, moral, and spiritual discipline is clearly back of the emergence of the Bible into history. Thus only can the Bible's existence be accounted for. What has not the Bible done in history since it came into existence? We meet it at every turn. In a very real sense it has made history. The Bible cannot be studied apart from history, nor can history be understood apart from the Bible. Produced by life, it in turn has made everything live whithersoever it has gone. And yet we exclude the Bible from education! Is there any need of support of our proposition and our protest? Witness the high estimate of the Bible by the masters in practically every department of high accomplishment. Can I better make a powerful plea for the Bible in education than by extensive quotation concerning it from masters in world leadership? Like responds to like. Deep calls to deep. Life recognizes itself.

The thoughtful, the true, the expectant, the adventurous, pioneers, pathfinders, the sacrificial, the suppliant—these flock together in scorn of time and space. No boundaries can keep them apart.

A SUMMARY OF SOME REASONS WHY THE BIBLE SHOULD BE IN EDUCATION

1. Its enormous contribution to the knowledge of universal human nature. It speaks to mankind in terms of essential humanity and in comprehensive variety of type. Its records of human experience, individual, family, community, national, social, international, are exceedingly rich.
2. Its geographical and historical values, and its stimulus to study of origins.
3. Its unsurpassable literary values.
4. Its widespread influence in human affairs, both past and present; also the assured prospect of continued and increasing influence in days to come.
5. Its lives of leaders.
6. Its life of the Leader of Mankind.
7. Its emancipating, releasing, liberty-giving values, together with its challenges to clear thought and noble action.
8. Its ethical and moral codes and motives.
9. Its ethic and interethnic values.
10. Its spiritual value. This constitutes its supreme value.
11. Its fundamental common sense. Read sample pages in the Proverbs, the Epistle of James and the Sermon on the Mount.

Immanuel Kant says: "The existence of the Bible as a book for the people is the greatest benefit which the human race has ever experienced. Every attempt to belittle it is a crime against humanity."

Lord Bacon says: "There never was found, in any age of the world, either religion or law that did so highly exalt the public good as the Bible."

Ralph Waldo Emerson says: "The most original book in the world is the Bible. Shakespeare, the first literary genius of the world, the highest in whom the moral is not the predominating element, leans on the Bible; his poetry presupposes it. People imagine that the place the Bible holds in the world it owes to miracles. It owes it simply to the fact that it came out of profounder depths of thought than any other book."

There is a charming reference to Emerson's contact with Carlyle at Craigen Puttock, Scotland, in his *English Traits*. Emerson says: "We went out to walk over long hills, and looked at Crippel, then without his cap, and down into Wordsworth's country. Then we sat down and talked of the immortality of the soul. It was not Carlyle's fault that we talked on that topic, for he had the natural disinclination of every nimble spirit to bruise itself against walls, and did not like to place himself where no step could be taken. But he was honest and true, and cognizant of the subtle links that bind the ages together, and saw how every event affects all the future. 'Christ died on the tree,' said he, 'that built

Dunscore Kirk yonder, that brought you and me together. Time has only a relative existence.' "

Carlyle's own words about the Bible, in part, are as follows: "The period of the Reformation was a judgment day for Europe, when all the nations were presented with the open Bible and all the emancipation of heart and intellect which an open Bible involves." Of the Book of Job he says: "There is no book in the Bible or out of it of equal literary merit." Here belongs Victor Hugo's estimate of Job: "Tomorrow, if all literature was to be destroyed and it was left to me to retain one work only, I should save Job."

"While the Bible has never numbered among its religious believers a fourth part of the human race," says Professor William Lyon Phelps, "yet it has swayed a greater amount of mind than any other volume the world has ever known. It has the singular faculty of attracting to itself the thinkers of the world as either friends or foes always and everywhere." He adds: "I thoroughly believe in education, but I believe a knowledge of the Bible without a college course is more valuable than a college course without the Bible. In the Bible we have the nature of boys and girls, men and women, more accurately charted than in the work of any modern novelist or playwright."

I shall insert here a summary of what the noted Jurist Wines, in his commentary on *The Laws of the*

Ancient Hebrews, says are the fundamental ideas at the basis of the Hebrew state. These he finds in the Old Testament portion of the Bible. I submit, are they not challenging to the educationalist? They are:

1. The unity of God.
2. The unity of the state.
3. Civil liberty.
4. Political equality.
5. An elective magistracy.
6. The sovereignty of the people.
7. The responsibility of Public officers to their constituents.
8. A prompt, cheap, and impartial administration of justice.
9. Peace and friendship with other people.
10. Encouragement of agriculture.
11. Universal industry.
12. The inviolability of private property.
13. The sacredness of the family relation.
14. The sanctity of human life.
15. Universal education.
16. Social union.
17. A well-adjusted balance of power.
18. An enlightened, dignified, venerable public opinion.

The words of Chief Justice Taft fit in here: "The classic English of the Bible has given shape to American literature. Its spirit has influenced American ideals in life and laws and government." So also those of Whitelaw Reid: "The Bible has been the basis and mainspring of Anglo-Saxon development for the last three centuries, having molded its morals, lifted its legislation and its jurisprudence, and inspired its literature."

Daniel Webster falls in line with a word to be soberly heeded: "If we abide by the principles taught in the Bible our country will go on prospering and to prosper; but if we and our posterity neglect its instructions and authority, no man can tell how sudden a catastrophe may overwhelm us and bury all our glory in profound obscurity." Webster is supported by Professor Edward König of the University of Bonn thus: "The guarding of the people's moral and religious interests is the greatest factor in the promoting of civilization." Hear also Chancellor Kent, one of the great jurists of America: "The general diffusion of the Bible is the most effectual way to civilize and humanize mankind, to purify and exalt the general system of public morals, to give efficiency to the just principles of international and municipal law, to indorse the observance of prudence, temperance, justice, and fortitude, and to improve all the relations of social and domestic life."

For further emphasis of literary values provided by the Bible, note the following: Edmund Gosse, the eminent English critic: "When young men ask me for advice in the formation of a prose style, I have no counsel for them except this—Read aloud a portion of the Old and another of the New Testament as often as you possibly can." Sir William Jones (familiar with the literature of twenty-eight languages—1746-1794): "I have carefully and regularly perused the Scriptures and am of the opinion that this volume, independent of its divine origin, contains more sublimity, purer morals, more important history, and finer strains of eloquence than can be collected from all the other books in whatsoever language they may be written." Richard Hurrell Froude: "The Bible thoroughly understood is a literature in itself—the rarest and richest in all departments of thought and imagination."

In this same line is a striking testimonial to the Bible uttered by Charles A. Dana, the late illustrious editor of *The New York Sun,* in an address at Union College to a graduating class of journalists. He said: "There are some books that are absolutely indispensable to the kind of education that we are contemplating, and to the profession that we are considering; and of all these the most indispensable, the most useful, the one whose knowledge is most effective, is the Bible. There is no book from which more valuable lessons can be learned. I am considering it now not as a religious book, but as a manual of utility, of professional preparation and professional use for a journalist. There is perhaps no book whose style is more suggestive and more instructive, from which you learn more directly that sublime simplicity which never exaggerates, which recounts the greatest event, with solemnity, of course, but without sentimentality or affectation, none which you open with such confidence and lay down with such reverence; there is no book like the Bible."

Professor Thomas Huxley is not popularly associated with indorsement of the Bible. In 1870 he made an address before the London School Board in advocacy of the reading of the Bible in the public schools. Of one of his statements quoted below (the one which mentions his perplexity) an observer remarks: "I think it is significant that necessity should force such a conclusion from him." Here are extracts from Professor Huxley's address: "I have been seriously perplexed to know by what practical measures the religious feeling, which is the essential basis of conduct, was to be kept up, in the present utterly chaotic state of opinion on these matters, without the use of the Bible. Take the Bible as a whole; make the severest deductions which fair criticism can dictate for shortcomings and positive errors; eliminate, as a sensible lay teacher would do if left to himself, all that is not desirable for children to occupy themselves with—and there still remains in this old literature a vast residuum of moral beauty and grandeur. And then consider the great historical fact that for three centuries this book has been woven into the life of all that is best and noblest in English history; that it has become the national epic of Britain, and is as familiar to noble and simple, from John O'Groat's House to Land's End, as Dante and Tasso were once to Italians; that it is written in the noblest and purest English, and abounds in exquisite beauties of mere literary form; and finally, that it forbids the veriest hind who never left his village, to be ignorant of the existence of other countries and other civilizations, and of a great past, stretching back to the farthest limits of the oldest nations in the world. By the study of what other book could children be so humanized and made to feel that each figure in that vast historical procession fills, like themselves, but a momentary space in the interval between two eternities, and earns the blessings or the curses of all time, according to its effort to do good and hate evil, even as they also are earning their payment for their work?"

Huxley near the end of his address continues thus: "That children take kindly to elementary science and art no one can doubt who has tried the experiment properly. And, if Bible-reading is not accompanied by constraint and solemnity, as if it were a sacramental operation, I do not believe there is anything in which children take more pleasure. At least I know that some of the pleasantest recollections of my childhood are connected with the voluntary study of an ancient Bible which belonged to my grandmother. There were splendid pictures in it, to be sure; but I recollect little or nothing about them save a portrait of the high priest in his vestments. What come vividly back on my mind are remembrances of my delight in the histories of Joseph and David, and my keen appreciation of the chivalrous conduct of Abraham in his dealing with Lot. Like a sudden flash there returns back upon me my utter scorn of the pettifogging meanness of Jacob, and my sympathetic grief over the heartbreaking lamentations of the cheated Esau, 'Hast thou not a blessing for me also, O my father?' And I see, as in a cloud, pictures of the grand phantasmagoria of the Book of Revelation.

"I enumerate, as they issue, the childish impressions which come crowding out of the pigeonholes in my brain, in which they have lain almost undisturbed for forty years. I prize them as an evidence that a child of five or six years old, left to his own devices, may be deeply interested in the Bible, and draw sound moral substance from it. And I rejoice that I was left to deal with the Bible alone; for if I had had some theological 'explainer' at my side, he might have tried, as such do, to lessen my indignation against Jacob, and thereby have warped my moral sense forever; while the great apocalyptic spectacle of the ultimate triumph of right and justice might have been turned to the base purpose of a pious lampooner of the papacy."

I should have quoted earlier the following from this same address: "I may add yet another claim of the Bible to the respect and attention of a democratic age. Throughout the history of the Western World, the Scriptures, Jewish and Christian, have been the great instigators of revolt against the worst forms of clerical and political despotism. The Bible has been the magna charta of the poor and of the oppressed. Down to modern times, no state has had a constitution in which the interests of the people are so largely taken into account; in which the duties, so much more than the privileges, of rulers are insisted upon, as that drawn up for Israel in Deuteronomy and Leviticus. Nowhere is the fundamental truth that the welfare of the state, in the long run, depends upon the righteousness of the citizen, so strongly laid down. The Bible is the most democratic book in the world. From the sixteenth century onward, the Protestant sects have favored political freedom, in proportion to the degree in which they have refused to acknowledge any ultimate authority save that of the Bible."

With these words put those of Horace Greeley and General Grant: "It is impossible to mentally or socially enslave a Bible-reading people." "The Bible is the sheet anchor of our liberties."

Is there not place here, before proceeding further, for the plea of Richard Moulton, author of *The Modern Reader's Bible,* for a place for the Bible in a liberal education? He says: "It has come by now to be generally recognized that the classics of

Greece and Rome stand to us in the position of an ancestral literature—the inspiration of our great masters, and bond of common associations between our poets and their readers. But does not such a position belong equally to the literature of the Bible? If our intellect and imagination have been formed by the Greeks, have we not in similar fashion drawn our moral and emotional training from Hebrew thought? Whence, then, the neglect of the Bible in our higher schools and colleges? It is one of the curiosities of our civilization that we are content to go for our liberal education to literatures which, morally, are at an opposite pole from ourselves: literatures in which the most exalted tone is often an apotheosis of the sensuous, which degrade divinity, not only to the human level, but to the lowest level of humanity. Our hardest social problem being temperance, we study in Greek the glorification of intoxication; while in mature life we are occupied in tracing law to the remotest corner of the universe, we go at school for literary impulse to the poetry that dramatizes the burden of hopeless fate. Our highest politics aim at conserving the arts of peace, our first poetic lessons are in an *Iliad* that cannot be appreciated without a blood-thirsty joy in killing. We seek to form a character in which delicacy and reserve shall be supreme, and at the same time are training our taste in literatures which, if published as English books, would be seized by the police. I recall these paradoxes, not to make objection, but to suggest the reasonableness of the claim that the one side of our liberal education should have another side to balance it. Prudish fears may be unwise, but there is no need to put an embargo upon decency. It is surely good that our youth, during the formative period, should have displayed to them, in a literary dress as brilliant as that of Greek literature, in lyrics which Pindar cannot surpass, in rhetoric as forcible as that of Demosthenes, or contemplative prose not inferior to Plato's—a people dominated by an utter passion for righteousness, a people whom ideas of purity, of infinite good, of universal order, of faith in the irresistible downfall of all moral evil, moved to a poetic passion as fervid, and speech as musical, as when Sappho sang of love or Æschylus thundered his deep notes of destiny. When it is added that the familiarity of the English Bible renders all this possible without the demand upon the time-table that would be involved in the learning of another language, it seems clear that our school and college curricula will not have shaken off their mediæval narrowness and renaissance paganism until classical and Biblical literatures stand side by side as sources of our highest culture." [1]

I beg to follow Moulton with a statement by my associate, Louis Matthews Sweet, in his study of the English Bible, where the historical significance of

[1] From *Literary Study of the Bible,* pp. viii, ix.

the Bible in relation to education is strikingly set forth: "It is to be remembered that throughout its entire course of development the people of Israel, however separated at the core by original ideas and principles of worship, was surrounded and pressed upon by the great nations of antiquity, who not only conditioned outwardly the movement of events in which Israel was involved, but formed the historical matrix in which Israel's national ideas and purposes were molded. Is it too much to assert that not a single line of the Old Testament would have assumed the form in which we have it, had it not been for the geographical situation of Palestine, which made Israel the frontier nation of the ancient world? No great nation of the Orient could look at another without sighting across the highlands of Judea. No nation could march against another without crossing Israel's territory or traversing her boundary. No more significant fact for the history of revelation could be imagined.

"In like manner the history of Christianity, from the advent of Christ on, was conditioned, in its modes of self-expression, in teaching and institutions, by the fact of its inception in the imperial era. It is a fact of history as well as of doctrine that Rome is the 'Babylon' of the New Testament.

"But there is another and still deeper reason why we are to consider the Bible to be the outcome of universal history, the product of universal Providence. No formal narrative of historic events in the various biblical eras could begin to give an account of the forces and influences which have gone to the making of the Bible. In its innermost essence the Bible is the response of the human spirit to the Spirit of God. While, in its immediate creation and publication, it is the outcome of that unexampled Hebraic sensitiveness to spiritual impressions which culminates in the world's supreme Teacher, yet, all the way along, the fact runs more deeply and spreads more widely than this exclusive reference to Israel would imply. The Bible represents the essential response of the human spirit to God as it represents the universal message of God to the spirit of man. There is throughout Scripture the deep undertone of universal humanity which is so much more than national consciousness or individual insight. That which is implied but not spoken, taken for granted but not formally inforced in Scripture, are those universal and fundamental convictions which are not the exclusive property of Hebrew or Christian, but belong to man, as such, made in the image of God. Without such a context and inwrought structure of universal principles, the Bible would be unintelligible. Therefore, the Hebrew priest, prophet, and sage, the Christian apostle and teacher, even the Lord Jesus Himself, each in his own order, spoke both for and to universal man, taking his stand firmly upon elementary truths acknowledged by all normally constituted men. Such being the case, by every implication of its nature and constitution the Bible is set in the midst of universal history which is its context, essential to the meaning of the text. The Bible cannot be studied apart from history."

Matthew Arnold's fine tribute to the Bible must have a place here. "To the Bible men will return because they cannot do without it; because happiness is our end and aim, and happiness belongs to righteousness, and righteousness is revealed in the Bible. For this simple reason men will return to the Bible just as a man who tried to give up food, thinking it was a vain thing and he could do without, would return to food; or a man who tried to give up sleep, thinking it was a vain thing and he could do without it, would return to sleep."

Time fails to introduce many others who belong to the goodly fellowship of the truly educated, whose tribute to the Christian Scriptures is hearty and large.

Why is it that of our modern education Woodrow Wilson dare say: "You know that with all our teaching we train nobody; you know that with all our instructing we instruct nobody." Or, President Nielson of Smith College: "We have no educational science, but several educational superstitions." If "the crowning achievement of the educator is the unification of personality," why not have our students include study into the secret of such unification in the heroes of Hebrew thought and life? What of the crowning personality? Let Judge Thomas M. Cooley, late professor of American history and constitutional law in the University of Michigan, answer: "I regard Jesus of Nazareth as having done more to advance civilization and to influence beneficially the history of the world than has any other historical character. The Bible I have been accustomed to look upon not as one book, but as many. The teachings of Jesus and his disciples, as given in the New Testament, I think constitute a book more important to the world and more influential in reforming and improving the conditions of mankind than any other."

Whittier may fittingly close this anthology:

"We search the world for truth.
We cull the good, the pure, the beautiful,
From graven stone and written scroll;
From all old flower fields of the soul;
And, weary seekers of the best,
We come back laden from our quest
To find that all the sages said
Is in the Book our mothers read."

THE PLACE OF WORSHIP IN RELIGIOUS EDUCATION

THE REVEREND JOHN WALLACE SUTER, JR., is executive secretary of the Department of Religious Education of the National Council of the Episcopal Church. He lectures on religious education and has given much emphasis to the place of worship in the church school. He is the author of *Creative Teaching,* a text-book used by many classes in training for teaching in the church school.

THE PLACE OF WORSHIP IN RELIGIOUS EDUCATION

By John Wallace Suter, Jr.

LET me begin by saying that as a general proposition I believe that in the religious educational program, worship should occupy a place corresponding to that which it occupies in religion. This raises the question of the place of worship in the Christian religion. Is it on the fringe or is it near or in the center? Where does worship fit in with the other things of the Christian's life, not only public worship, but also private prayer? If we can think that out for ourselves and come to some agreement about what place worship should occupy in the normal life of a Christian, we shall be ready to make up our minds what place training in worship should occupy in the religious educational program for children and young people.

The worship of Almighty God is the main thing in the Christian life, the heart of the whole matter. In fact, if you skim through the history not only of the Christian religion, but religions in general, you will find that wherever a religion is persecuted people give up everything, if they have to except worship. To this they cling tenaciously, even if they are driven into catacombs or other secret places to hold their services. There seems to be an instinctive feeling that worship is the main thing. If you had to tear down some of your church property for one reason or other, and were allowed to keep only one unit of it, I am inclined to think that you would let everything else be torn down but the sanctuary where people address themselves to God.

Now as I look over the actual practices in church work I sometimes fail to see a recognition of these truths. Personally, I like to think of a church school in a parish as being an organization or plan or scheme or program which surrounds the sanctuary or church—that is, the place where we worship. Let us not call it an auditorium. What does the word auditorium mean? It connotes a listening-place where the people in the seats are passive and do nothing but observe other things being done. An auditorium properly describes a room where people gather when they go to see a play or hear a concert. In the auditorium the people are listeners or spectators of what takes place on the platform. The transfer of the term auditorium from the secular field of the theater and lecture-hall to the church is one of the greatest verbal calamities that has happened to Protestant Christendom in the past few years. It gives the whole thing away. Unconsciously you think you come to church to watch someone else worship, just as you go to the theater to watch someone else act.

The church building proper should not be called the auditorium, but the "church." It is that holy place where we meet together for the most sacred things of life: the blessing of baptism, and, for the other end of life, the funeral; the joy of the marriage service; the gathering around the Lord's table to receive the Holy Communion. That hallowed place should be central to the whole religious educational program. The classrooms should exist on the fringe, around the altar, chiefly to interpret worship; to tell a child why he comes to church, why he hears the Bible read; to explain where the Bible came from, who wrote it, etc., so that the child can go to church with more joy, devotion, and intelligence. When the child goes to church he hears hymns sung and takes part in singing them, and needs to know what they mean; and so with the prayers and other forms of worship. There are many things that need to be explained so that the child can enter into them more naturally, and these classrooms make it possible for the children to enter with heart and soul and mind into the main business of the Christian religion, which is doing something toward God.

Now of course there are other things. I like to think of religious education as consisting of three main enterprises. The first is worship, as you have already guessed. The second is serving our fellow-men. Every parish should provide for its boys and girls a carefully worked out program by which they can perform generous acts for fellow human beings, not only for those they see, but for those who live at the other end of the earth—a program of generous, purposeful activity for others, wherein they can give of their time, money, and skill. The third is the search for truth. These boys and girls have a right to know, and must be helped by us to seek out, the truth. Here is this universe in which we live and which God made. Any fact that we can help them find out about it is a sacred fact, because, if it is a fact, God made it so. There is no such thing as secular knowledge. To a believer in God all knowledge is sacred. There are no frivolous facts. God did not make the serious facts and some imp the funny facts. Every fact is a part of His purpose. If water freezes at the temperature of 32 degrees Fahrenheit, that is a sacred fact because God thought it up and created it. Everything they learn in day schools which is true is sacred and is of God.

These children come to church and ask when? and who? and what? We have to help them in their search for truth and encourage them to ask questions and help them to answer them in the true spirit, so that the church-school classroom may supplement the things that the children learn in the day schools. Of course, it is a great pity that we cannot conduct all their education in one. The right way for us as Christians would be to have the church teach our children secular knowledge; but there are many reasons why we cannot do this at the present time. It would be ideal for the church to teach its boys and girls everything they have to learn —arithmetic, reading, writing, etc.—and mix it all in with religion, helping the children to see that there is only one universe and one God, and that no two truths can ever contradict each other.

I think we would all agree that worship is something that we do toward God. Its peculiar character comes in these two words, "toward God." When we study about him, we talk about Him in the third person singular, God does this and God does that. But in worship we talk *to* Him, in the second person. We come together in groups, in a room designed for the purpose, and lift up our hearts toward Him in unison, using certain words that link us with the past and also with all other living Christians. We perform these exercises of the soul, stretching upward toward God, and we do these things *en masse*. Those who have studied the psychology of it find that when people get together in one mind and with one accord, and in one theme address God, the psychological atmosphere of that group changes, and things happen which could not happen if each one did it by himself. There is a psychological change whenever people come together to address themselves to God.

If I were going into a church school for the first time, perhaps taking charge of it for a year, I should of course watch the school and go around and see what was being done. Supposing the school were in a pretty bad state and ineffective and blundering. The first thing I would do would be to set in order its public worship. I would get that fixed and have it straightened out if it took a year. I am convinced that a school that has fairly good classroom work and good teachers, but which does not have anything significant going on in worship, is on the whole wasting its time and effort. I would put the worship to rights first and see that every boy and girl in the parish had a chance to go to a beautifully-conducted service of worship where he himself could approach God and praise Him. When I had that going so that it meant something in their lives, I would begin to think of picking out a group of boys or girls and sending them to a classroom before or after this service of worship, where they could find out the reasons for the things done in worship. Here they would be assisted by teachers. In time I might have a number of such classes, but *only after* the heart of religious education had been properly cared for by a properly conducted service of worship. So many churches play with little imitations of worship.

This does much harm and counteracts the good which may be done in the classroom.

Some of you have been in religious educational work long enough to know that various things have been put in the center. Not many years ago the whole school revolved around the Bible, and was even called a "Bible school." Now there was a lot of good in that, and it matched pretty well the day schools of those days. The day school was a book school and most of the day-school learning was done by rote. I am not criticizing it for those days. Besides, look what was produced! Here we are; some of us are not so bad. It had its day. Then came a change, and psychology became a little more scientific. Presently we had a time of putting the child in the center of the church-school curriculum, and it seems to me that that was an advance because it matched the period. We built a child-centered curriculum. I should think the child would have died of self-consciousness. We cut him up and down and right and left, and formed the curriculum to fit the child; and in that, as also in the Bible-centered curriculum, there was a good deal of sense. Certain communions and certain churches have put the church in the center, and that has its good points and its bad points. It depends on what you mean by church. Of course, each age thinks it is right, and if we are relativists we know that pretty soon there will be another age which will have it more nearly right.

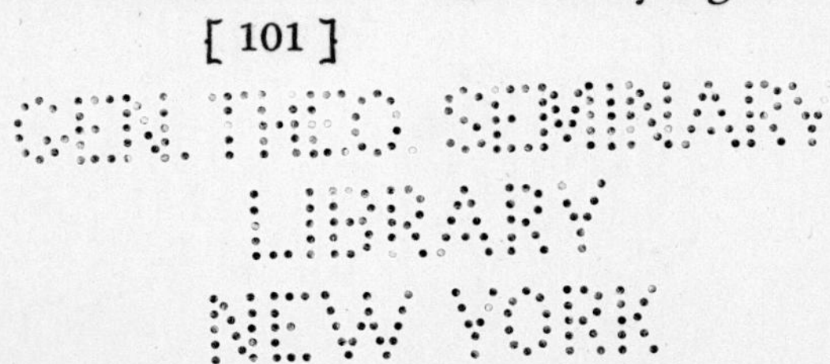

What I am advocating now is putting God in the center. It is the only thing that matters. We must think of each boy and girl and ask ourselves this question: "What effect is my school having on this boy or girl with respect to his or her relation to God?" We have been saying, "What effect has this school on this boy?" But I want to rivet attention on what effect this school has on the boy *in respect to this boy's relation to God.* It is all right to teach him how to draw neat maps and see how he improves from September to June, but our school does not exist to make him an expert cartographer. What I want to know is, what influence has God upon that boy's life? If that boy is influenced more by God in June than in September, I want that increasing influence to be what my school has helped to do for the boy. The whole point of the religious life is to put people into a position where their hearts and souls are open to the play of the Spirit upon them, so that God will be helping them make their choices and thus leading them into acts of purity and honesty and kindness and so on. That is what it is all about, and nothing but God should be in the center of our curriculum and efforts in religious education.

Now that is why the old-timers were really right. When they put the Bible in the center, they meant God. I am making a collection of the points at which modern religious education is very like the old, and here is one of the points. Some of us have been rather poking fun at the Bible school. But these people meant God, and had the right idea; only their age fell into an extravagant notion of literal inspiration.

Today we talk about a curriculum of experience, in which I for one thoroughly believe. In my mind the curriculum is not a set of books. It is a series of experiences into which we entice the children. The experiences are examples of purposeful activity, experiences toward God, very largely experiences of worship. That is what the curriculum must be—a series of Godward experiences. It can be Godward if it involves serving other people in consequence of having worshiped God, and as a test of the sincerity of our worship. We can serve Him because of our desire to do His will and to grow in His image.

Some "projects" in religious education are not projects at all. If it is going to be a real project, it must have God at the center; otherwise it is not religious education in the true sense of the phrase.

Our children, I believe, should go to church every Sunday to worship God. I would make that an absolute rule. Is your Sunday-morning time-schedule the best it can be? Is it such that every child can go to church for a really significant service? The worst we can do is to give them a little half-hour imitation of morning worship before their lessons and then hustle them back for another little imitation. That is zero. It is much better to do nothing at all than that. Another plan, which is much better of course, is to assemble the whole school once in the church itself for a real service of twenty or twenty-five minutes, carefully planned and conducted by a clergyman or someone specially set apart, really well-conducted with as much attention to beauty as the regular service would receive—and then send them into the classrooms. Another scheme is to have all the children, if there is room, come to church with their parents and stay for the first half hour, then march out into the adjoining building and have their lessons during the period of the grown-up sermon, so that all the people, young and old, are being instructed at the same time.

There are six or eight different time-tables being used by different churches today. The point is that only that time-table is good which provides serious and carefully planned worship for every child once every Sunday. There is something wrong if you are not giving that much to your children.

Of course I would like to discuss the contents of these services, but that is a long story. I suppose that we would agree that what the liturgists call the "notes" of worship must all be present in the course of a year. Thanksgiving is one of the characteristic attitudes of the soul toward God. Penitence is another. Praise is another. And there are half a dozen more. The point is that each service shall have a central theme, like Thanksgiving, for instance. The hymns and readings and prayers should all bear upon a single theme. Another point is that the people in the pews are the ones who are supposed to do the worshiping. The minister, whoever he or she may be, is put there in order to induce the people to praise God and worship Him. There are several ways of doing that, and it involves a knowledge of liturgics and psychology.

Here is a test question for you to put to yourself. It is an imaginative one. Try to pretend you are a boy or a girl of ten or twelve, and that you have just been to church, to the service you usually go to on Sunday morning, and you come out through the door and on the way home are asked this question, "What do you feel that you have been doing?" It would be hard to make children answer frankly, but if you could get a frank and accurate answer from one, in too many cases he would say, if he were articulate enough: "I have not been doing anything; I have been somewhere and endured something. I have met an engagement. I was sent there and stayed through it and possibly had two minutes of enjoyment because I had a little fun on the sly." The way the child ought to feel is that he has exercised a part of his being and that he was the doer, and he ought to feel tired in a way—the same kind of fatigue that you feel after you have been to a gymnasium and have exercised your muscles, the ones you don't use in the ordinary course of the day, and it makes you feel better and breathe deeper. The church service should be something like a spiritual gymnasium where the soul, in company with other souls, goes through an exercise and stretches itself Godward and really does draw near to God and increases its strength a little bit. And so when the child comes back he should be able to say: "I have been approaching God and seeking our Father. I have been doing it with the other boys and girls." And now in your respective church schools, how do you think they do feel? Do they feel exhilarated and spiritually "set up" in consequence of the spiritual exercises they have been engaging in?

One of the greatest skills in the world is that of conducting public worship for children. I hope you have in your parish someone who knows how to lead children in worshiping God, a person who is consecrated and skillful in that particular work. If you have, that should be his (or her) job for the parish, and don't you dare let him do anything else!

WHEN IS EDUCATION RELIGIOUS?

ADELAIDE T. CASE, PH.D., is assistant professor in religious education in Teachers College, Columbia University. She is a graduate of Bryn Mawr College and holds a Ph.Degree from Columbia University. Miss Case is active in the Federal Council of the Churches of Christ in America, the Religious Education Association, the National Student Council of the Young Women's Christian Association, and the National Student Council of the Episcopal Church. She is the author of *Liberal Christianity and Religious Education.*

WHEN IS EDUCATION RELIGIOUS?

By Adelaide T. Case

It is one of the most encouraging signs of progress in religious education that a group of teachers and religious leaders should come together on Saturday mornings to discuss fundamental questions underlying all their work. No one who has been in touch with the movement for many years, as I have been, can doubt that there has been a distinct change of direction and deepening of interest in recent years. Ten, or even five, years ago, we discussed devices and details, and considered such questions as departmental grading and whether plasticine was good material for children to use. Such matters are of importance, but it is of immense significance that we are now giving more attention to the basic principles that must determine our choice of methods and materials.

The question "When is education religious?" has received four typical answers, each representing a major emphasis in everyday practice. Education is religious:

I. When the Bible is being taught.

II. When ideas of God are being shared and the experience of God is induced.

III. When character is being developed in the direction of Christian ideals.

IV. When the teacher possesses a religious personality.

The great difficulty with religious education is that many of us are in danger of treating each of these answers as if it were complete and final in itself. We have been operating, so to speak, on a one-tube set. All of these emphases are needed. They must be combined, both in theory and in practice, if education is to be religious, in any effective sense. Let us take up these answers separately.

I. A large number of people regard teaching the Bible as the primary purpose of religious education. Sometimes, however, this Bible-centered teaching is carried on without sufficient appreciation of the other emphases suggested. From the point of view of character education it sometimes leaves much to be desired. At times it fails to induce an experience of the Christian God. To be sure there are difficulties in Bible-teaching which expose us to dangers which should be faced.

The first difficulty is due to the practice of using the Bible to thwart rather than encourage ethical judgment and discrimination. We have allowed children to infer from our teaching that there is nothing to criticize in many if not all of the Old Testament characters. Solomon has been described as a model monarch, not only wise, but just and kind, whereas we know that, in spite of the wonderful prayer at the beginning of his reign, he was an oppressive and cruel tyrant. We have not helped children to develop critical appreciations based on the standards of Jesus. We have sometimes "played up" dramatic incidents and ignored character values. Elijah, for instance, has been presented as a magician and hero of violence, but his moral earnestness has been neglected.

Another danger into which liberals especially fall is that we shall teach the Bible without moral purpose. Not long ago a friend told me about a young theological student who was asked to teach a Bible class of cleaning-women in a downtown mission. These women worked very hard, but they were religious people and they were willing to come once a week to study the Bible. The young man went down to meet them and opened the first session in this fashion. "I understand," he said, "that you want to study the Bible. Now, just which Bible do you want to study?" Of course they were very much bewildered, but finally one of the women summoned up her courage and said, "Well, sir, I'd like to begin with John because I have found great comfort in that Book." "Fine," he replied. "We'll begin with the Gospel of John, but of course you must realize that it was not written by John the son of Zebedee." And with that he launched into a discussion of the

Johannine problem. None of the women turned up for the second session of the class.

This kind of Bible-teaching is ineffective because it is not filled with moral purpose. As an element in religious teaching critical study of the Bible has an important function, but it must be subordinate to human values.

A third danger in our use of the Bible is that we may leave our pupils with an inadequate idea of God. Unless we are careful, children who are brought up on the Bible are almost sure to have not one God, the God of our Lord Jesus Christ, but a number of different gods—the god or gods of the early Canaanites; the god of the wandering Hebrew tribes, the god of the Babylonians whose religion the Israelites accepted to some extent when they were in captivity. No wonder that children's religious experience is often so naïvely primitive or hopelessly confused!

Recognizing these difficulties, how can we make our Bible-teaching strongly religious? By being positive at those very points where a negative attitude has wrought such havoc. We have all met people who argue that we should give up teaching the Bible because it has been so unsatisfactorily taught in the past. If that were to be our test, we ought to abandon various fields of education, including the history of our own country! Surely, what we need to do is to continue our use of the Bible—for our children must have the records of Christianity and its long background in Jewish history and culture—but courageously to reconstruct our teaching at those points where it now falls short.

To suggest the practical directions that such reconstruction must take, I should like to bring before you a few concrete experiences.

On ethical discrimination: Recently I met a college friend whom I had not seen for many years. She has four children and she was telling me something of her ideas in regard to their religious education. She believes ardently in teaching the Bible from the time that they are very small, and finds very little difficulty. One of her children, about seven years old, said to her, after hearing the story of Abraham offering Isaac: "I don't think that was nice of God. I think that Abraham really knew more than God." Of course my friend followed that up. She was not shocked; she was glad to hear it. She was centering her attention on the Bible, but she was encouraging ethical discrimination.

On teaching the Bible to meet situations on a Christian level, that is, with moral purpose: A class of third-grade boys and girls were looking at pictures of the life of Christ, when one of the children said something derogatory about one of the pictures, "I don't like Jesus in that picture," or something of that kind. "Oh, you mustn't say that!" exclaimed another child. "God will punish you." The whole class stopped for a breathless moment, thinking not about Jesus, but about the punishments of God when one hurts His feelings. "Does God ever punish people?" the teacher asked. "Yes," they unanimously agreed (and this was a progressive church school!). "He sometimes kills them; He sends floods; He makes them sick."

"You know," said the teacher, "I wonder if God really does things like that. Some people think he does, and when Jesus was alive many people thought that God punished people. But I don't think Jesus thought so. Anyway, he told his friends this story about God." The teacher then related the story of the Prodigal Son, reconstructing it a little from the point of view of the expectation of punishment on the part of the son, and his surprise when he saw his father running out to welcome him. When the story was over, the first response was from a boy, who said: "That's just like my mother. She doesn't always punish me when I've been bad." And several of the children wondered if God could be like their own mothers and fathers, a God of love and forgiveness.

On the Christian idea of God: The illustration just given also bears on this point, although it was told largely to show the value of using the Bible to meet a classroom situation. As another illustration, I want to share with you this testimony from a girl in the seventh grade, who had been studying the

Bible from the point of view of the Christian experience of God. It is a letter written to an imaginary friend in India.

"Dear Friend,
Our religion is called the Christian religion which means followers of Christ. There are many Christian churches each having different beliefs, but most of the big ones are universal. We believe in a God who is everywhere and in our hearts. It is He who comforts us in our troubles and helps us in our hours of need. He is a God of love and not of war and strife. We are His people and the sheep of His pasture."

We must never be content with our Bible-teaching unless it gives our children the Christian conception of God, showing how this conception developed step by step through the long experience of Jewish history.

II.—Other people say that education is religious when it is concerned with ideas of God and experiences of fellowship with Him. This group insists upon the importance of carefully planned worship for children and is relatively less interested in Bible-teaching and character education. As I go about the country I find a considerable number of people who want to give up the church school entirely and substitute for it a children's church, where services are held on the basis of children's needs and interests. Some leaders advocate the establishment of "children's corners"—portions of the church that are set apart for children's private and corporate devotions. Others are enthusiastic about bringing children into the regular services of worship intended for grown people. They would "revive the family pew" even if it meant the disappearance of the church school. All these teachers and preachers are alive to the importance of emotional factors in religious education. Moreover, they are certainly right in reminding us that if the worship of God is in reality the central act of our lives, we must learn to guide children at an early age into full participation in this experience.

As a complete program for religious education, however, this insistence on the importance of worship is not without its dangers. One of them lies in the shallowness of religious emotion without historical reference. We must not allow our children to forget that their experience of God has its roots in an ancient past and that their faith—as Protestants if you will—must be based, not on dogmatic formulas or intuitive assumptions, but upon certain historical facts, primarily the life of Jesus as recorded in the Bible and the story of His forerunners and followers up to the present day. I wonder if we are not now witnessing in American Protestantism a certain wave of religious emotionalism that is partially responsible for this emphasis on worship—fine in itself but quite futile without a strong factual and intellectual background.

Another and more insidious danger is the disintegration of character resulting from a worship that is divorced from definite ethical teaching. Even worship that is apparently satisfying to leaders and children often suffers at this point. When I visit church-school services, a grave suspicion often assails me: can these children grow in Christian character through this story or sermon, these hymns, prayers, Scriptural passages? What is the connection between this worship and everyday problems?

Over and over again I have thought of that story of Phillips Brooks with which you are probably familiar. Although he had been brought up in a religious family, young Phillips Brooks was not in the habit of "free prayer" in public. Soon after his arrival as a student in a Southern theological seminary, he was invited to attend a class prayer-meeting. He could not bring himself to take any part in it, but he was filled with admiration of the fluent and beautiful petitions to Almighty God that some of the other boys offered. What was his consternation next morning in Greek class to realize that the students who were unprepared to do the translations assigned were the very boys who had been most voluble in prayer the night before!

Again, we must beware of the danger of not giving children enough responsibility. We want active pupils, not passive devotees, but we have inherited a tradition of worship that puts children in a relatively passive position. The leader directs the thought and the group follows. Docility is at a premium.

In pointing out the dangers associated with this view of religious education, I do not want to leave you with the impression that it is not preëminently our task to develop a vital fellowship with God. What I do want to emphasize is that fellowship with God must have historical background; it must include Biblical-teaching; it must make for character development.

As an illustration of a religious education which has been adequate in the experience of God that it has suggested, read these verses written by a thirteen-year-old girl as one of the elements of a service of worship.

GOD IS LOVE

"Yes, truly, truly, God is love,
A spirit that is always near,
A friend in whom one may confide
And love without a single fear.

"For God is with us here and now
In all the little things we do,
In kindness and in sacrifice
One sees his love shine through.

"He helps us overcome our faults,
To helpful be in worldly strife,
To give up cheerfully the best,
To go unselfishly through life.

"The God of olden Bible days
He was an Emperor, a King,
A Lord who lived in palaces
With all that earthly wealth could bring;

"God is our Pal, a helpmate dear,
He never was a King above;
He loves us, helps us, gives us all.
I tell you God is love."

III.—Many religious liberals declare that education is religious when character is being developed, especially when the elements of Christian character are being built into the everyday lives of children. We all have a fairly clear idea of what is meant by Christian character. We think at once of high qualities of courage, self-control, and perseverance, readiness to take responsibility and to meet emergencies, widening of fellowships and the breaking down of prejudices, sacrifice in devotion to a great cause. Let me frankly say that those who conclude that religious education is largely the development of character are in danger of selling out as teachers of religion to the character-education enthusiasts.

Let us consider some of the difficulties involved in identifying character education with religion.

One difficulty, as I see it from the point of view of practical teaching, is that character education without the idea of God lacks a unifying concept large enough for a satisfying integration of personality. Moral conduct easily tends to break up into an aggregate of separate habits. It tends to be focused upon relatively narrow aims of vocational efficiency and nationalism. Both of these tendencies need to be offset by conscious reference to the supernational and supernatural will of God with whom we may have an invigorating fellowship.

Another difficulty, in practice, is that our emphasis on character education is in danger of being insufficiently historical. It cannot have perspective either in the past or in the future unless it is associated with the study of the long moral struggle of the race. This means, of course, religious history, for in the past—if not in the present—religion and morals have been intimately connected. We need the Bible. We need to have the biblical account extended up to the present day. Without such historical study this emphasis on character education will give us a sort of plane geometry of life, without depth or solidity.

Let me, however, add that as religious people we ought to rejoice in the researches done in the name of character education and in the stimulus that they bring us to show forth our faith "not only with our lips, but in our lives." They should constantly remind us that the religion of the Hebrew prophets and Jesus was, unlike many of its rivals, profoundly ethical in its nature.

IV.—The last answer, that "Education is religious when the teacher has a religious personality," has much to commend it. We all agree that Christian people must teach our children the Christian religion. We could all supply instances when men and women of transparently noble and simple character were far more successful as religious teachers than professionally trained mediocrities. We probably know many mothers who say to us, "I'd rather have Mary spend half an hour studying arithmetic with Miss Smith than half an hour in church school with Miss Jones; it does her more good." We must take care, however, that our children's religious development is not dependent upon their relation with one person; it must not be bound up with one set of personal adjustments. Moreover, since the Christian religion involves intelligence as well as good will, the teacher should be prepared to use religious history with discriminating appreciation and to introduce to her students some of the complicated problems of modern life. And that means some measure of professional training. We thus answer our question in too narrow a fashion if we say that education is religious when the teacher has a religious personality.

Nothing is so seriously needed in the movement for religious education at just this point in its development as an effort to keep steadily before us these four answers to the question, When is education religious? We must make practical use of all four answers; we cannot afford to lose a single one of them out of our working policy. A well-balanced program of religious education must include Bible study and religious history. It must include an adequate presentation of the idea of God and experience of fellowship with Him. It must include emphasis on character education. It must, of course, presuppose a religious personality as teacher and friend.

Where can this all-around religious education best be carried on? Obviously, not in the public school, although there we can find many elements of religious education and a constant testing-ground for our success or failure. I confess that I am not very sanguine about the possibilities of the ordinary church school with its short sessions, artificial atmosphere, and conscripted teachers. Very little constructive teaching can be expected in the modern home. If we are to go forward, we must look for a new leadership in the church. Surely the time has come for the churches to set up a seven-day plan for religious education which will utilize the public school, the home, the playground, and the church school, integrating the religious aspects of all these experiences and directing them toward the realization of Christian purposes.

SOME SOCIAL OBJECTIVES OF RELIGIOUS EDUCATION

BENJAMIN S. WINCHESTER, D.D., is executive secretary of the Commission on Christian Education of the Federal Council of the Churches of Christ in America. He was formerly assistant professor of religious education at Yale University. He is a lecturer on religious education and the author of several books: *The Youth of a People; The Master Teacher; Religious Education and Democracy.*

SOME SOCIAL OBJECTIVES OF RELIGIOUS EDUCATION

By Benjamin S. Winchester

As ONE looks over the material that is provided for courses of study and text-books in religious education, he is impressed by the fact that the emphasis is very strongly, almost exclusively, on the individual. We say that in preparation for teaching we must study the child. When we speak of methods, we think of them as means to bring about certain changes in the child. Our emphasis, particularly in these later years, has been upon the individual, whether child or young person, because for so long we had given almost exclusive thinking to the lesson material.

Of course, in the last analysis, the individual is the ultimate unit and we are all individually responsible. That is our religious point of view and we are trying to make individuals realize their responsibility and act accordingly. And yet we must take into account, in all our teaching, the fact that we do not live in a vacuum. We are social beings and the way we act at any given moment is very largely determined, not by the ideals which we may hold as individuals, nor by the system of ideas which we happen to have, but by the kind of people we happen to be with at the time. It would therefore seem that we ought at least to give consideration throughout our whole plan to the social aspects of behavior and to the social relationships of the persons we teach.

Recent psychological study has given us a sound basis for this social emphasis. Consider for a moment two or three of the more typical theories. Take, for example, the point of view of those who are interested in heredity. The eugenists are rather a discouraging group so far as educators are concerned. They make one feel that education is a hopeless task. Here we are, and how we get here is no affair of our own. We simply cannot help ourselves. These persons give a good deal of support to those who insist that human nature cannot be changed. They tell us we are conditioned by our endowment at birth and that we cannot change; what we are depends upon what our ancestors were; and this is illustrated by the Jukes family and the Jonathan Edwards family.

This is all very well and much of it is quite true. We all have our physical and mental limitations from which we cannot altogether escape. Yet, these writers prove a little too much. If Jonathan Edwards had an array of brilliant descendants, it is possible that this may have been due in part to the fact that they were brought up in Jonathan Edwards' family as well as to the fact that they were born of

Jonathan Edwards. We are reminded also that as we go back ten generations each one of us has some thousands of great-grandparents. Possibly among these many people there were, besides thieves and robbers, some decent persons. So we need not be discouraged overmuch by this talk about heredity. Let us make of it all we can. But the important point for us to keep in mind is that heredity has social significance. In our very origin we are the product of social relationships, and these have everything to do with what we are.

Consider next the much-discussed school of psychology, known as the behaviorists. Professor Harrison S. Elliott in his interesting little book, *The Bearing of Psychology Upon Religion,* points out that we should distinguish between the behaviorist as a psychologist and the behaviorist as a philosopher and theologian. This is a very important distinction. What has the behaviorist been trying to say to us? One thing is that character is very largely the result of the way we respond to the world about us, including our fellow human beings. The behaviorist and the eugenist are a long way apart. The behaviorist builds up personality in all its complexity out of the multitude of responses we make. But he makes of this a very mechanical process, so that man becomes a kind of push-button. Quite aside from this mechanistic aspect of the theory, the behaviorist does emphasize the fact that what we are, and what our pupils are, depends very largely upon the kind of people we are with. They help to make up our world; we act toward them, and with them, and we react together toward the world around us. Whatever we may think of behaviorism on other grounds, this is something we should keep in mind as we try to teach. If education is an emotional conditioning of our reflexes, it makes a great deal of difference whom we are with during the process of conditioning. What happens in thus being together is that the group is being educated and its members are educating each other.

There is another theory that has become more or less popular, whose catchwords we find everywhere—that of psycho-analysis. At first glance, the psycho-analyst seems to be at the other extreme from the behaviorist. To the behaviorist everything is on the surface, so to speak. In trying to make a science of psychology he limits the field of his study to those objectives which lie open for everyone to observe. The psycho-analyst also tries to be scientific. But he asserts that what we see on the surface is not character; the springs of character are below the level of consciousness, down in the mysterious depths of the subconscious mind. That is where we need to go to find out what a man is and what he is likely to do and be. So we hear a great deal about the conflicts that go on within us, keep us out of sorts with the world, and make us feel edgewise toward one another. We have to get at these and resolve them into their components if we are going to be happy and make others happy.

Again let me point out that a great deal of what a psycho-analyst has to say is of social import. Whether we are exuberant and enthusiastic people or whether we are morose and shirk off into a corner, depends to a great extent upon the way we have been treated by somebody else—in short, upon the whole mass of social relations we have had. We need not go further into the discussion of psycho-analysis than to note that its advocates insist that we are educated by our social relationships, in them and for them. For example, children are born into the family group. In this group their characters are largely determined by their relation to one another and to their father and mother. As they go out from the home into the school, they enter a new world. Between the world of the family and that of the school there is usually more or less of conflict, and it is the part of some person to help adjust these conflicts. Again there is the self-formed social group, the gang, with its own code of morals. And there is the social group in the conventional sense, the political group, the industrial group, each of which has its own way of acting. The teacher's business is to help people live in a consistent fashion in all these groups, to show them how to follow a consistent purpose through all of them, to enable individuals to make themselves effective in all groups so that they carry along the rest of the group toward the fulfillment of a common purpose. Social adjustment is to be brought about through the enlistment of the members of the group in a common purpose. Or, speaking as one interested in religion, social adjustment is to be achieved by group-discovery of the purpose of God, by objectifying that purpose, by making it so definite and concrete that one can see in a particular situation just what it means and follow it out by the enlistment of the whole group.

What we ought to do as teachers is to grapple with some of the social problems which confront us today. There are a number of them and some are very acute. I remember hearing a man not very long ago make a very eloquent address in which he pointed out the difficulties which we face today. He spoke of the industrial problem, the prevalent lawlessness, the so-called crime wave, the breakdown of the family, the difficulties that young people get into, the menace of war. He said that if we believe these things ought to be done away with, we must support and contribute to the cause of religious education. All of which one could assent to very warmly. But, from the point of view of the hard-headed business man, he left out one link in the chain. He did not show just how these things would be taken care of by religious education. He assumed that if we support a program of religious education, therefore we shall automatically do away with war and lawlessness and intemperance and vice. The business man would say that this does not necessarily follow unless in our program of education we drive at this particular thing, and find out what kind of education will make people law-observing and behave in the family and keep peace with one another.

It therefore seems worth while to consider some of the great problems of society today and ask ourselves what we are going to do about them.

Take, for instance, honesty. We speak of "common honesty." One gets the impression from the newspapers that honesty must be very uncommon. And yet it is common. Most people are honest—at times. A friend said recently that he had discovered in a certain school that some of the pupils were stealing from one another. They did not call it by that name. They just took things, and the school authorities were very much surprised to learn of the stealing because the school had an honor system and it was very seldom that anyone was caught cheating in the particular situations which the honor system covered. But the matter of stealing was a different question. Now we sometimes get the impression that by a kind of blanket term we can cover all our relationships in society, especially if we learn the name of an attitude so that we can speak it glibly on occasion. We hastily assume that it stands for everything that might be brought under that name. The psychologists tell us that this is not the fact. There is no such a thing as "transfer" in anything like the degree that we have assumed it to take place. A "trait" of character is simply the name we give for convenience to a large variety of our reactions to a certain type of situation. In speaking of honesty we have tried to bring a great many things under that term—truth-telling, the unwillingness to cheat, unwillingness to steal, the insistence that one will never be anything other than what he actually seems to be at the time, and many others. How do we train for honesty? We are apt to do this simply by general teaching, and delude ourselves by thinking that if we teach children to be "good," they will be honest. This may be an exaggeration, but we may well question whether we are anywhere near as definite in attempting to teach honesty as we ought to be. The work that Professor Hartshorne and his colaborers are doing will perhaps help us to make over our whole scheme of training on this point, and will compel us to study afresh our procedure by bringing it to bear upon all those typical experiences which boys and girls have, at the primary age, the junior age, the intermediate, and so on. We must help our youth to confront these beforehand as far as they can, and to grapple at the time with the problem as to whether they will be honest or not in these various kinds of situations.

We must bring to them at such times considerations which seem to make it worth while for them to be honest. Now these would be social situations. One cannot be honest merely as an individual. Honesty involves relations with others. There is a great field here for the cultivation of honesty which grows with experience and as we meet with and decide new problems.

Again, there is the problem of industry. How many of our boys and girls in this highly industrialized age are being given opportunity to take an intelligent and Christian attitude toward the problems of industry? For the most part, is it not true that the children of manufacturers are brought up with the children of manufacturers? Of course some of them go to public school, but many go to private schools. The children hear their parents talk about manufacturing from the point of view of the manufacturer. They hear about profits and strikes and the other things that are problems of the manufacturer. Conversely, the children of employees are apt to grow up with the children of employees and hear about the difficulties of labor and the oppression of the capitalists. Thus these two groups are being educated away from each other. What provision have we for helping both to understand the whole situation? Miss Peabody, of the Auburn School of Religious Education, has worked out a very interesting course for juniors on The Christian Idea of Work, in which she has tried to help children, some of them perhaps for the first time, to experience what it means to create something, to realize that things belong to us when we have actually made them, and especially if we have created something that will be of social value. Here is a very important idea. What is the Christian view of work and wealth? What are we doing to help young people to have such a view, with full sympathy toward the man who works with his hands, and also toward the man who works with capital, so as to realize that both of them should be servants of their fellow-men?

Then there is the problem of temperance which has taken on some new aspects in these last few years. We did try some years ago to teach people temperance. We had lessons in the public schools about the effect of alcohol upon the human system, and in church school we had occasional lessons about the evil effects of strong drink. These did a great deal of good and helped to create a generation of people who hated the saloon, because its abolition was the objective toward which we were working. They helped to do away with that institution with all its incentives to the forming of bad habits and its social and political implications. The saloon has gone as a legalized institution. What are we aiming at now? We cannot keep attacking the saloon, now that it is outlawed. The bootlegger is not quite so easy to locate as the saloon was, and, moreover, there is a good deal of remonstrance, especially in the cities, against the whole situation created by prohibition. It has become not merely a question of temperance now, although it is still that, and we are not even saying much about temperance to our children. We stopped that when the Eighteenth Amendment was passed. It has now become also a question of law observance, and it is on that point that the social group is especially in great need of education. Should everyone unquestioningly obey the law? There are many people today who say we should not. What is the law? Why is the law? When should one obey the law? When has one the right to defy the law? These are real questions, and we are not getting any very effective systematic education regarding them. It is a social question involving the whole relationship of a person to society. Has society a right to restrain the individual, and if so, under what circumstances? Of course if one starts out to kill people, society will stop him if it can. But, apart from such extreme cases, how far has society the right to dictate to the individual? Society says that a person can drive an automobile too fast. Suppose a man is under the influence of liquor and drives an automobile. Has society anything to say about that? There are a thousand situations which boys and girls and older people face where we need an education shot through with the religious motive. What is the purpose of God for society? How can we unitedly achieve that purpose, and where does law come in?

And then there is the great question of peace. Quite a good deal is being done in this field. Recently an interesting group, representing fifteen or twenty different church agencies of education, seriously faced the problem of how to bring about peace. Some of these agencies had courses of study on peace, some had discussion courses, some had books upon the subject, and some had activities to suggest. What is peace? Peace is that condition in society and in the world at large when individuals in a group, and groups of people in their relation to one another, have found a way to settle their difficulties and conflicts according to justice, the golden rule, and according to reason, rather than by force. To be sure, peace does not inevitably follow when we have given some general instruction in religion. We must give boys and girls practice in their small groups in settling their difficulties. We need to set up machinery between groups, whether they be industrial or political or national groups, by which these conflicts may be adjusted. A little book like that by Mrs. Bonser on *The Golden Rule City* illustrates what may be done with a junior group in the working out of community relationships on the basis of the golden rule. This book teaches peace, although the word peace seldom occurs in it.

Finally, take the problem of the family in its social relationships. With regard to the question of sex relations, the word "sex" suggests to many minds the stories of crime which cover the front pages of the newspapers and the sensational titles of plays and movies—in a word, the perversions of sex relations. Is it not strange that as Christian people we overlook the great importance of sex as a factor in education? It ought first to suggest the tenderness of mother love, sisterly devotion, the strength and sympathy of fathers, and the noble chivalry of brothers. How could we have these things without sex? Why do we not make more of these possibilities? Why do we not realize that in our teaching of religion these fine things which come out of sex relationships may be lifted up and refined and used to ennoble the characters of our boys and girls? Sex education ought to mean the taking of these natural social relationships and making them as fine as they ought to be. All of the impulses which we have in our ordinary life may lead to degradation. It is the business of education to beautify them.

We have only touched upon the possibilities of utilizing social relationships in education. In the weekday schools especially we have a splendid opportunity, for in our weekday classes we are as yet fairly free from traditional procedure. Why cannot we persistently and systematically aim at the solution of some of these great social problems, begin to solve them by developing socially minded groups—groups on which certain habit systems of group action will be built up, groups that will seek to realize the purposes of God and to create a Christian society? If we could make these the main objectives of weekday schools, we should go a long way toward meeting some of the difficulties which arise when we ask what is the relation of the weekday session to the Sunday session, or to the public school, or to other educational programs.

LEADERSHIP ATTITUDES AS PRINCIPLES OF EDUCATION

JOSEPH M. ARTMAN was a pastor in Chicago before he held positions in the University of Chicago as director of vocational training, and as professor of religious education. Since October, 1926, he has been general secretary of the Religious Education Association, which has for its aim, "To inspire the educational forces of our country with the religious ideal; to inspire the religious forces of our country with the educational ideal; and to keep before the public mind the ideal of religious education and the sense of its need and value." He is one of the authors of *Undergraduates.* A study of Morale in Twenty-three American Colleges and Universities.

LEADERSHIP ATTITUDES AS PRINCIPLES OF EDUCATION

By J. M. Artman

FOR more than fifteen years I was professor in the Y. M. C. A. College and in the University of Chicago. During those years I gave much time to selecting and advising leaders in all sorts of religious educational enterprises. These leaders worked in many types of agencies—in churches, colleges, universities, in public schools and Christian associations, in social settlements, playgrounds, and camps, with Scouts, Camp Fire Girls, and the like. After this experience with leaders of many types and degrees of ability, working in a great variety of situations, I have come to the conclusion that success in religious educational enterprises *depends more upon the basic characteristics or attitudes of the leader* than upon all other factors combined.

In speaking of characteristics or attitudes, I am not thinking of abstract theories, untested hypotheses, or something apart from the leader, but of qualities, traits, or mindsets. These are the fiber and tissue of the leader's life—his methods of living and thinking. They are tied up with the individual leader, of course, but they also involve the educational agency through which the leader operates. The situation is bilateral in nature—the leader on the one hand, and the leadership agency on the other—the leader working in and through the agency, the agency helping or holding back the leader in his work. Much of this paper is devoted to the basic characteristics of leaders as applied to these two aspects of the subject.

I

First of all, note the necessity of the leader recognizing the bilateral nature of leadership. The fact that practically all leadership is bilateral (if not multilateral) in nature needs to receive great emphasis, for it has not been generally or intelligently understood. It is an interesting fact that when a leader fails, employers lay responsibility for the failure upon the employee. It seems that executive psychology operates on the assumption that the employee is always wrong. The executive often makes the employee a scapegoat for his own sins. In most experiences of this sort, I have scarcely ever known an executive to assume responsibility for the failure of an under worker. Nevertheless, there can be no great leadership development until we recognize the fact that back of the employee is the presence and power of the employing agency or individual, and that he is often at least fifty per cent responsible for success or failure.

Experience has led me to the conviction that an alert diagnostician can literally bank on wholesome outcomes when desirable qualities are present in the leadership situation, or can predict failure when a wrong kind of mindset prevails in either employer or employee.

I know many situations where mindset in the executive, principal, president, dean, pastor, or chairman is such that no leader, working under or with him, can possibly carry through an effective educational program. Administrators in such situations are often dominated by motives of self-interest, getting funds, or politically satisfying the whims of persons whose favor is needed. This is not meant to infer that it is impossible for a creative and dynamic personality to break through almost any type of staid situation if his attitude and methods are right. It is meant that the odds are against him unless his employer is purposefully sharing with him in the enterprise. When the proper mindedness pervades both the leader and those responsible for him, success is largely insured and educational results follow. When, therefore, the bilateral nature of leadership is taken into consideration in the original set-up, and both leader and agency are together ready for purposeful questing, the process is accelerated and certainty of wholesome educational outcomes is greatly enhanced.

An educational leadership situation thus involves not only the leader, but also the institution which employs him, with its traditions and trends; the board and administrators with whom he is to work; other workers, if any, coequal, above, or below him in status; other agencies or institutions in the community; the social and intellectual status or condition of the group with which he is to work; the financial status of the institution; and the total community situation.

Many of the most tragic failures I know have been made by bright persons who were exceptionally well trained from the school point of view, but who did not have an adequate perspective of what leadership involves. Such persons did not see that a vital part of the educational leadership lay in the groundwork preparation of developing wholesome attitudes between themselves and their employers, and with other persons with whom they were associated. Esprit de corps between the leader and all others having contact with the learning process involved is absolutely essential before the leader's own educational task can be successfully achieved.

I want to protest against any agency or institution that, having secured the best trained leader possible, puts him into a stultifying, mordant situation where there is no hope of realizing educational progress or retaining his own moral vigor. Let me give you a few illustrations which point out the tragedy of such situations.

There is a religious educator in a large city church whose pastor has refused utterly to enter heartily into a united church program. This lack of coöperation has gradually put religious education into a little corner in the church program, and has actively worked to influence the official board and congregation in such a way as literally to squelch the religious-work director. He was partly to blame. He should have surveyed the field before accepting the call and in a prophetic manner pointed out what was involved in his contemplated relationship. In like manner, the pastor did not know what was expected in the leadership program of his church. Neither the pastor nor the religious educator had been trained to diagnose an educational situation and prescribe a program that would aid those whom it would interest, and offer opportunity for leadership and growth for the leaders who shared in it.

In common with other agencies (church, college, public school), the Y. M. C. A. has gradually come to consider all of its work as a religious educational opportunity. Under the older program "religious educators" were employed and placed in a religious section paralleling departments of physical education, boys' work, etc. The conception that religious education could be a qualitative phase of all activities had not yet been developed. This new conception, which views all activities as potential opportunities for religious education, is rapidly being adopted in significant Y. M. C. A. programs. Mr. Glen O. Pierrel, who five years ago was employed as Metropolitan Religious Work Director for the Y. M. C. A. in Chicago, has brought about so great a change in the philosophy of the work that his title has been changed to Metropolitan Program and Research Secretary.

While this newer conception of the program has been officially recognized, the older corps of leaders, habituated to promote innumerable programs, activities, and stunts, are retained. Most of these men have not been trained as educators. Hence, when a dynamic religious educator is employed, who has notions of stimulating all activities to become religious, serious clashing between the various secretaries arises. Each seems to have a "claim" or a "pasture" of his own with which no one else should meddle. The administrative officers often have no greater, and sometimes have less, understanding of religious education than department secretaries. Hence, time and again the general secretary has supported the view that religious education is a thing in itself—meetings, special classes, dormitory stunts, specialties—and has made the work of the religious educator and of religious education itself impossible. The psychology of factory production dominates.

Other complications are often found wherein donors and board members definitely use the institution to maintain the *status quo* rather than as an agency for releasing religious living. Secretaries argue that it is not in their province to have ideas on industrial, economic, or political problems that find expression in functional manner. Thus the "Y" service is largely ameliorative and non-creative in face of economic situations that call for the daring of a social prophet.

I do not want to appear to single out the Y. M. C. A. as differing greatly from other agencies. In many respects it is ahead of church and college. Take an illustration from the university world:

A very prominent state college has in the last ten years unseated three presidents by means of political intrigue carried on by state officials and a few members of the faculty. Regardless of the justice of either or both sides of these quarrels, the result has been that the mouths of professors who wish to continue in their positions have been very effectively sealed. In this college political manipulations have thrown a fear complex into practically the entire faculty, so that the moral and spiritual heroism of faculty members is effectively suppressed. The really strong professors have either left or are quietly trying to find a way to go. The new professors coming into this kind of scene soon find an overhanging condition that threatens to deprive them of their own good judgment. At first they are baffled, and soon are either forced to retire from the institution or else choose nonentity in so far as being of particular force. The strange thing here is that the employing agency has made the success of the faculty, from a moral and spiritual standpoint, practically impossible. This means that the student body is not only left to shift for itself, but the faculty condition disseminates disquietude and acts as a spiritual hazard for the students.

It is easily understood how security of position, especially when the professor has a family to care for, may become his dominating motive. The suspicions and threatened discharge brought about by political factors, or any other underhanded manipulations, produce quiescence in an otherwise morally and spiritually dynamic professor.

Another college has recently gone heresy-hunting to such an extent that each professor is asked to sign a theological statement which makes open, frank expression of opinion impossible. The trustees of the same institution recently accepted a gift with such theological conditions attached as bind them to the necessity of treating their faculty as bad boys. These bad boys must be bound by strict promise not to go out of certain bounds, or not to do certain things, or else the trustees themselves will be acting in bad faith with the donor by keeping actual conditions on the campus hidden. The president of the institution, in an interview, intimated that the latter policy would perhaps be followed. It is easily seen that no self-respecting professor can live a genuinely moral and spiritual existence under such conditions. Nor can any professor possibly have a real spiritual influence on students under conditions as provided by this institution.

It happens, therefore, that the bilateral nature of leadership—employer and employee—is often the deciding factor in leadership success. I am of the opinion that in many institutions this factor greatly overshadows the so-called conflict between science and religion with its disturbing tendencies. Professors by the hundreds have chosen, consciously or unconsciously, to be pure scientists (and hence leave moral and spiritual issues alone), solely because of the mordant leadership situation under which they are forced to work.

The recognition of the unique significance of the bilateralness of leadership becomes, therefore, one of the essential characteristics in a real leader. One's relations to his colaborers is a primary condition for successful approach to the learner. The leader who does not perceive this has demonstrated striking unfitness for leadership.

II

Experience has taught me that the lesson-minded purveyor of courses and subjects, whose one and only interest lies in passing over his wares to the learner and watching zestfully to see that the learner does not cheat in the process of parroting it back to him in recitations and examinations, is a positive menace to human society. He should never be placed in leadership positions until he has experienced a genuine conversion from dead knowledge, or perhaps more truly a conversion from a dead to a living use of knowledge. This is true no matter whether he is a comparatively untrained person or a highly-wrought-out Ph.D. His lesson-parroting, fact-worshiping approach to learners, whether in primary school or college, deadens all zest for living.

On the other hand, the person who has caught the vision of living dynamically, who has a passion for helping folks find themselves as agents in growing human enterprises, not only must use knowledge, but must hold it as a jewel to be prized. If he has tact and good sense, he will always be a center of zestful, dynamic living.

May I give an illustration or two to throw these types in bold relief: Here is a teacher of a boys' church-school class. In a two-hour tram ride this teacher poured out his heart in search for some formula to get his boys to behave. "What can I do to make these boys keep quiet and take interest in the lesson?" He told how he worked eight hours a day in a downtown office, traveled back and forth two hours, used an hour and a half for meals. "But," said he, "I love to study my lesson and never give less than an hour a day to it." "What about the seventeen boys? Where were they in this scheme?" I inquired. The total picture revealed that this teacher of lessons did not know all the names of the seventeen boys in his class. He did not know the kinds of homes from which they came, having never visited any of them. He knew nothing of where or how or in what the fathers worked, nor whether the mothers worked, what the family standards and ideals were, what reading material was in the home and what the family read, where the boys played, with whom, and under what circumstances, what they did in school and what they liked and disliked there. He knew one thing only—to teach lessons—and this he loved. He knew nothing of the legion problems and difficulties of these boys. All this rich material was wholly foreign to his mind. He was making religion, which might have been life itself, merely a stupid lesson to learn. As an escape from such stupidity, the boys threw wads, pinched, stuck pins—anything to get a bit of activity to escape from such dullness.

The number of folk attempting this sort of leadership is legion. The holder of a professorship of Bible in a college, who stresses facts, facts, facts—whether a Ph.D., B.D., or what not—is in this category, and is a positive hindrance to wholesome living. The leader who has discovered the sheer joy of releasing folk into worthful human living is an altogether different person. He is interested in living itself, and in the persons who are learning to live. He uses knowledge, to be sure, often in greater quantity than the lesson purveyor, but he uses it to solve some human issue, and not just for the sake of grades, examinations, or diplomas. A student in a graduate school recently said, "Well, I'll spend my Fourth of July conjugating Old English verbs. Isn't that a Fourth for you?" he added, with a distasteful twist of his face. "Well, but why do it if you dislike it so?" "Have to. The university has always required it for the degree. The professor frankly says it is a waste of time, but regulations are regulations."

I am convinced from many such experiences that the Herbartian notion of knowledge for knowledge's sake, which so captured our educational theories and schemes in the past two or three generations, is responsible for much of the stultifying leadership to be found in idea-centered preachers, lesson-gorged religious educators, subject-minded college and school faculties. The volume entitled, *Undergraduates,* just published, reveals the fact that the great motive for extra-curricular activities on the part of students has been their irrepressible demand for reality as over against stultifying knowledge-dosing. Yes! The lesson-minded person is to be shunned. Knowledge is real when it becomes insight for rich, pulsating living.

III

The mindset in a leader's loyalties just as keenly betrays potential strength or weakness. A keen diagnostician of leadership can easily decide whether the leader is loyal to himself—to "me and my wife, my son John and his wife, us four and no more"—to a certain group or gang, to a psychological theory, to a fixed set of ideas like fundamentalism or modernism, to a board of directors, to a denomination. Sometimes a leader's loyalties do not locate in either God or man, but in a certain set of ideas or a subject. After teaching Old Testament in an institution for twenty years, one is very liable to demand the continuance of the course in the curriculum forever, for no other reason than "It must be—it is *my course.*" A certain widely known leader first began in the Y. M. C. A., then changed to Scouting, then to church-school work, then to another form of work. In each instance he formed severe and demanding loyalties to the particular work in which he was engaged. No one else's work counted.

Another widely known leader works in many situations, but sooner or later turns everything to praise and acclaim for himself. He even demands that the institution through which he works give acclaim to him as the one and only leader, for the present at least. This man's work, in consequence, becomes a stumbling-block and a blight on wholesome living.

Is the leader loyal to the Kingdom of God? Does he and can he be depended upon to "love God rather than man," whether in the presence of humble living, bishop, potentate, or king? Is he loyal to Jesus? And is he loyal to Jesus by living in the strength of Jesus in current human issues, or by lip service and belief in the dogmas about Jesus? Can the deeds of his certain loyalty be clearly traced through the pulsing issues of his active life? If there is no record of sacrifice "even unto death" for the issues of life, then one has a right to discount the sincerity of his leadership. Certainly faith in him is severely shaken if his loyalties are lip loyalties only.

Here, for example, is a college president who exhorts his faculty and students to serve. Yet it is common knowledge that he subsidizes his football team with his left hand while preaching righteousness with his right.

Loyalties are rather quickly revealed by the company one keeps—either with present folk of power or with those of the past. From whom does the leader draw inspiration? With whom does he wish to share life's efforts for righteousness? Self-love, small and trifling group love, is not a mark of strength in leadership, whether in a bishop or in a leader of Boy Scouts. The love of God which passeth understanding is a safer guide.

IV

A further consideration for understanding a leader's worth is his attitude toward causes or issues of living. It is worth noting that all great souls have given their lives in behalf of causes. Indeed, no leader ever becomes really and vitally trustworthy as a leader except by giving himself in behalf of causes. A Lincoln, a Wilson, a Mott, a Jane Addams, a Rabbi Hirsch can be catalogued rather easily. The ordinary person is ordinary, it seems, because he does not give himself in behalf of a cause. And even when interested, the leader is so often interested merely in knowledge of a cause, or a desire to talk about it, rather than to do something about it.

Let me illustrate the opposite of this tendency: I have had opportunity to observe closely the originator of the outlawry-of-war notion. At first he buttonholed everyone who would listen; brought small groups together in his home to debate the question; read every treatise he could lay hands on about the whole business of war; gathered clippings from world-wide sources; wrote many letters, fostering and seeking opinions; talked law and international law to senators and representatives and to the President of the United States. He interchanged views with European leaders; prepared plans by which the matter could be consummated; encouraged others to write and speak in its behalf; stimulated resolutions in Congress and spent a vast amount of his own money on the project. When one follows the activities of this man in behalf of this cause, one is not at all surprised to see him become a potential world figure within a few years. And those who worked with him, who spoke or wrote on behalf of his cause, participated to some degree in the same growth. It appears that a cause carries the person in its wake as well as lays bare his qualities of leadership.

Since all causes are specific, it helps in diagnosis to catalogue the issues to which the leader under observation has given his efforts. To what causes has he responded within the past five years? What do these reveal regarding the type of issues to which he is sensitive? Are they of real moment or inconsequential? Leaders who tend to the inconsequential issues are not to be trusted.

Several other tendencies of leaders relative to causes quickly reveal dependability or the lack of it. Among these are good or bad judgment, the vital or indifferent use of knowledge, the actual responses in resolving the issue, and whether the leader is coöperative or single-handed in his efforts. Has the leader's experience and intelligence been such that he can be trusted for good judgment in the face of any issue? Does he seek for and get the knowledge essential for good judgment? Does he insist upon full or partial knowledge? Does he really do something about the issue, or does he discuss it and bring nothing to pass? Does he prefer to work alone, or does he easily and naturally ally himself with others? The tendencies shown in these practices in behalf of causes quickly reveal whether he is reliable as a captain of righteousness.

V

The leader reveals wholesome or unwholesome characteristics in his attitude toward change. We are living in a changing world. Kilpatrick holds that the leadership task is "Education for a Changing Civilization," to quote the title of his book. This fact of change lies at the very heart of creative leadership. It is quite revealing, therefore, to find whether the leader is attempting to transfer fixed standards, norms, rules, doctrines, to the learners, and accordingly trying to make it impossible for them to change; or whether he is interested in stimulating wholesome change which perhaps may even redirect the course of change itself. The real leader is alert to trends, foresees essential changes, is ready to trade horses in the middle of the stream, so to speak, if need be, and yet is poised, making judgments safe enough for himself and others to bank upon. It is true, therefore, that not only is sensitiveness to change essential to the leader, but also that he plan his efforts toward making the change meaningful, powerful, creative.

May I call your attention to the fact that in this rapidly changing world, in which wholesome change is essential for the continuance of any civilized life, the majority of text-books on religious education, as well as most plans and programs, are devised for the purpose of causing people to resist change? The major objective of the leaders who prepare materials and tools of education, in both content and method, is to develop the type of person who will not change. Anyone who follows such doctrines, who looks upon modes of religion as unchanging laws to obey, does not fundamentally appreciate the nature of human life.

There are many other phases of this problem that should be studied. Further attention should be given to the positive and negative characteristics displayed by the leader in his seeking after and use of knowledge in resolving issues, to his characteristics in the giving of good or bad judgment. Much more should be said about his tendencies to do something positively and surely about human issues and causes.

A great deal could be said about the tendencies of some leaders to have confidence or lack of confidence in the ability of folk. Many leaders fail because their work is not inspired by a fundamental conviction of the educability of people.

WEEKDAY RELIGIOUS EDUCATION

CHARLES H. TUTTLE, A.B., LL.B., is well known as lawyer, author, statesman and member of the Board of Trustees of the College of the City of New York. He is United States District Attorney for the Southern District of New York. His great interest apart from his profession is in Religious Education. For many years he has been Chairman of the Religious Education Committee of the Greater New York Federation of Churches. He was Counsel for the Federation and the New York State Council of Religious Education in the Freethinkers suit. He is a Director and one of the Founders of the Religious Education Foundation. He is the Superintendent of the Church School and a vestryman of St. Luke's Protestant Episcopal Church, New York City.

WEEKDAY RELIGIOUS EDUCATION

By Charles H. Tuttle

THE minds and hearts of our country at this time are turned to its richest endowment,—the American child.

We who are adults face the fact that a vast army is moving to take possession of all that we and our nation have built,—our institutions of learning, our pulpits, our banks, our business houses, our offices of government, and even our homes. This army is coming, as numerous and inexhaustible as the sands of the sea, with banners flying, and faces brightened with the hope and courage of youth. In their ranks are the new captains of the future, the new leaders of thought, the new helmsmen of government, the builders of tomorrow. As we watch the coming of their far-flung lines, we know how truly civilization advances on the feet of children, and how deep is our own responsibility to fit them to cherish and further the best in all which we ourselves have been able to accomplish.

Thus our coming army directs our thoughts not only to education but to religion. Education and religion belong together. They have the common task and end of fitting the individual more perfectly to his environment, in order that he may have a more abundant life. Their difference is solely one of emphasis, for perfect education must teach that which is true and beautiful and good, whereas religion, pure and undefiled, must teach that which is good and beautiful and true. As said by the great philosopher Thomas Huxley in words quoted by Herbert Spencer: "True science and true religion are twin sisters, and the separation of either from the other is sure to prove the death of both, for science prospers exactly in proportion as does religion; and religion flourishes in exact proportion to the scientific depth and firmness of its base."

The supreme aim of both education and religion is the building of character. Education which has its end in mere erudition is not only imperfect, but it carries the sinister implication that mere knowledge, and not the stewardship which knowledge imposes, is the aim of living. On the other hand, religion which fails to beget the loyalty to eternal principles, the good-will and the self-governing capacity which make up moral character, soon loses vital contact with and spiritual influence over life.

Today, the practical value of character is realized as never before. The vast structure of modern society and government is so complex that it cannot rest on the basis of an honesty which is regarded solely as a luxury, and not as a habit. Even in terms of each, nothing counts so much as character. According to the figures of the National Surety Company, whose business it is to insure business, property worth three billions of dollars will be stolen during the next twelve months. In the United States the annual cost of crime, direct and indirect, is ten billion dollars,—a sum which if devoted to education or to religion alone would build three ten million dollar colleges or cathedrals a day, indefinitely. This staggering cost falls, directly or indirectly, upon every business and every home in the community. Hidden in the expense account of every merchant is the influence of every dishonesty in the community.

We hear much talk today concerning gross materialism, increase in crime and unruly youth. But personally I believe that faith was never at such a flood tide as today. It may not be an organized and indoctrinated faith; but it rests upon an enlightenment which gives to religion a firmer basis and grander scope than ever before conceived. Our present difficulties are due to the fact that during the last few decades political, material and scientific advancement have proceeded at a terrific pace, without a corresponding increase and organization in spiritual forces. The solution of the problem lies in catching up; and this can be accomplished only as we again bring religion and the great moral verities for which it supplies the only rational sanctions.

into more vital participation in the life of the new generation.

Hence, Religious Education comes to us as a bugle call. It invites us to look upon the child not as merely so much animation, with a stomach to fill with food and a head to fill with information, but as a spiritual being to be fitted to the environment of those moral principles which condition abundant life here and hereafter and which are the necessary reflections of a moral universe.

This work cannot be accomplished by attempting to throw it off on the public schools. They can aid, but they cannot replace in primary importance the home and the church. The public school is America's unique achievement and America's proper pride. It is democracy's necessary guarantee of equal mental opportunity for all. But the Church should be the first to support the American people in their insistence that in the public school there be no sectarianism, either of religion or of irreligion. To introduce formal religious instruction into the public schools would be a long step toward the destruction of the freedom of the Church, for it would put religion under the control of the State. Nevertheless, the public schools,—and, indeed, all secular schools,—can add to character something more than the discipline of instruction, and can so teach children as not to let the state decay and civilization dissolve. They can teach character by arithmetic, when they present the science of numbers as the symbol of accuracy and truth. They can teach character when they represent language as saying what we mean,—"yea, yea and nay, nay." They can teach character when they represent history as preaching the gospel of a common humanity and a gradual evolution toward Human Brotherhood.

But the secular schools cannot proceed otherwise than by indirection. Indeed, their program of secular study has itself so enormously expanded in recent years as to leave little standing room at all in the life of the child for religion, and it has come to include subjects such as biology, sociology, ethics, civics and psychology,—subjects which enter those fields of origins and of destiny, of human conduct and relationship, with which religion is vitally concerned. Hence, on the one side, modern secular education tends to absorb to itself the entire educational capacity of the child; and, on the other side, it makes necessary consideration of the interpretation which modern education puts upon its own subject-matter, for upon that interpretation depends the question, vital to the individual and the nation, whether our youth shall be taught that religion and God are baneful superstitions, or that they are merely negligible, or that they supply the most beautiful and ennobling thing in life.

The problem, therefore, is to find, amid the demands of modern secular education and of the flaming allurements of modern life, a larger and an adequate standing room in the life of the child for religious education.

Such larger standing room must find its beginning in the home. While millions of American children are ignorant of real home-life, there are millions of others upon whom the home can, if it will, stamp the conviction that religion has a genuine message and a high purpose for them. If the atmosphere of the home subtly conveys the thought that it makes no difference whether one lives honestly, whether one does one's work or shirks it, whether one is kind or unkind, whether one has reverence or not for the Father of all Good, then those who make the home must not be astonished to find that the children run to the worst things instead of the best. In a garden, it is the weeds, and not the flowers, which grow without attention; and yet it is the flowers which add to the liveliness and purity of life. Virtue, like other beautiful things of the spirit, needs cultivation; and no means of cultivation equals that genuine religion which conceives the universe as merely a larger home and all in it as the common children of One Father.

A larger standing room for religious education is also being supplied by the movement growing rapidly among the churches for Weekday Religious Education.

A great door of opportunity for this movement was thrown open by the decision of the Court of Appeals of the State of New York rendered in May, 1927. By holding that for an hour a week children in the public schools could lawfully be excused upon the request of their parents to attend upon religious instruction at such centres outside the school as the parents designated, the Court granted a charter of liberty to the parents and schools of the state and to religion. That decision touches the whole of American life. It has rejected principles which were capable of consecrating secularism as the religion of America. It has protected the innermost shrine of liberty by vindicating the right of parents to participate in guiding the education and nurturing the souls of their children. It has preserved to the schools themselves a way of escape from the sectarianism of irreligion.

This movement to find a larger standing room in the week for religious education is coöperative rather than solely parochial. It is designed to stimulate community interest in religious education by giving it as much as possible the authority of a community undertaking; and it attempts to demonstrate to all children that, whatever may be the divisiveness of adult sectarianism, the heart of the child presents a platform broad enough for religious unity. These weekday schools are held after public school hours, and in some rural communities children are excused from the public schools at the request of their parents for one hour a week for attendance at such religious schools as their parents may designate.

It is this movement which holds the hope of the future, for however adequate the Sunday School may have been when life was simpler, the average Sunday School is not sufficiently dynamic and has not sufficient time to make headway against the material demands and attractions of modern life. But the Weekday Church Schools are the small beginnings of a greater movement which will lead the Church to take up religious education as a major enterprise. Too often the Church seems to treat religious education as a casual, intermittent and altogether subsidiary undertaking,—a secondary and wholly junior consideration, a thing of the basement, of haphazard direction, and of parochial rather than of nation-wide concern. In short, although youth is the best endowment fund which the church has, there are times when the church seems to treat the religious education of youth with a certain condescension. Although in its youth the church possesses high-powered ammunition sufficient to blow down the gates of hell on earth, it sometimes acts as if afraid to touch it, and as if an adult-program were safer. The growing movement for weekday religious education is the commencement of a new attitude and the expression of a new conviction; and if in this the churches fail, and keep on failing, religion as the dominant force for righteousness may vanish from the earth.

Moreover, with such a failure would go the security and greatness of the state. Precisely as a democratic state must as a matter of self-preservation equip its voters with intellectuality, so likewise the continued existence and development of democracy require that every individual in the state shall have moral and religious training. A nation's destiny is not in its learning or in its scientific attainments. It is in its character. The heart of culture is the culture of the heart. Our nation cannot survive materially unless it is preserved spiritually. Mere intellectual growth will never sustain our form of government unless it is accompanied by a moral growth; and there is no source of moral power comparable to that spiritual interpretation of life which is religion in its essence,—religion pure and undefiled. We shall surely perish in the muck of fleeting material sensations and the amassing of money, unless we can understand, and have our children understand, that life is more than raiment and is to be lived nobly according to the dictates of a lively moral and religious sense. The voice of patriotic statesmanship as well as of human experience in all ages, gave its true verdict in the words of George Washington when he said in his immortal Farewell Address:

"Let us with caution indulge the supposition that morality can be maintained without religion. Whatever may be conceded to the influence of refined education on minds of peculiar structure, reason and experience both forbid us to expect that national morality can prevail in exclusion of religious principle."

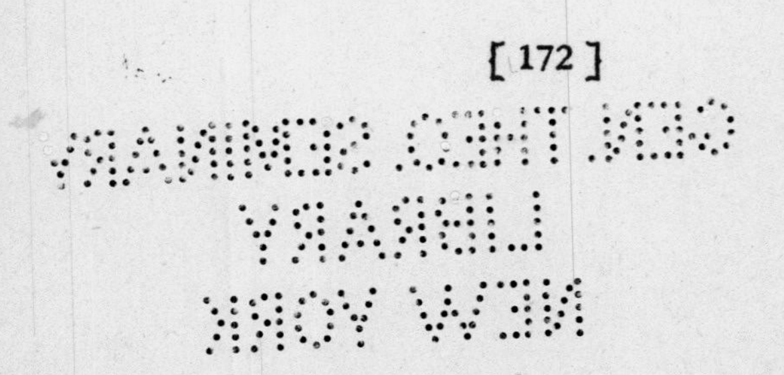